Book of American Furniture

Made by
John Townsend
Rhode Island
1765

Book of
American

Furniture

Doreen Beck

HAMLYN
London New York Sydney Toronto

Published by
The Hamlyn Publishing Group Limited
London · New York · Sydney · Toronto
Hamlyn House, Feltham, Middlesex, England

© Copyright The Hamlyn Publishing Group Limited 1973
ISBN 0 600 31292 5

Phototypeset in England by
The Siviter Smith Company Limited
Printed in England by
Sir Joseph Causton & Sons Limited

Contents

2   1

1 *Drop-leaf table with raked legs and butterfly brackets—a cherry and maple specimen from Connecticut where the butterfly wings seem to have been invented. Because of its rarity and uniquely American quality, the butterfly table has probably been faked more often than any other type of early table.*

2 *Transitional country armchair with new-style (Queen Anne) back and old-style (William & Mary) leg and stretcher turnings. This one recently fetched $1,000 at auction—about £400.*

3 *A maple slat-back armchair painted black. This Pennsylvania specimen recently brought $1,500 at auction—some £600.*

Introduction

Numbers in the margin refer to illustrations

It will no doubt come as a surprise to many readers to learn that a peculiarly American idiom exists in furniture styles. They shouldn't feel too guilty. Ever since the beginning of this Republic–the United States, that is–arrogant European critics have wandered over and cast scorn on the very notion of anything 'American', and in general Americans themselves did not begin looking appreciatively at their furniture heritage until well into this century, the very idea of a cultural heritage being somewhat suspect to the descendants of all those rugged individualists who had tamed a wilderness.

Interest in the past had certainly been stirred at the time of the country's Centennial celebrations in 1876, but by the turn of the century only a very small band of people had become curious enough–or crazy enough, it was then felt–to start collecting things actually made in these United States.

The treasures of one of those crazy early collectors came to rest in New York's Metropolitan Museum, and in 1924 they were put on display in the country's first American Wing. Collecting American had become respectable, and a fresh impetus was given to the age-old search for roots, and for the legend, tradition and romance attached to the pretty things from the past. In 1929 several months before the financial crash on Wall Street, the country was startled by the prices paid at auction for vintage American craftsmanship. Collecting American had also become something of an investment.

Today interest in American furniture among other domestic arts is widespread, and prices are back up in the stratosphere–at least for the best pieces. American Wings can be found in museums across the country and period furnishings figure prominently in an ever-increasing number of restorations–houses, villages, a whole town in the case of Williamsburg, Virginia, restored to the way they looked at some point in the last three or four centuries.

4 *Late 18th-century walnut kas from New Jersey. The older form of this piece was retained down into the 19th century.*

MADE AND SOLD BY
MATTHEW EGERTON, Junior,
JOINER and CABINETMAKER,
NEW-BRUNSWICK,
NEW-JERSEY
—No.

5 *A rare and therefore very precious label from the New Jersey kas.*

The White House itself was not unaffected by the search for an American past and several of its rooms have now been restored with among other things American furniture, to the way they would have looked when Thomas Jefferson or Abraham Lincoln was Chief Executive. In future any furniture shipped out of the House will be deposited in the Smithsonian Institution and not on the auction block as was common practice in the 19th century. Over the last decade or so a number of the Diplomatic Reception Rooms at the State Department, America's Foreign Office, have also been furnished with American pieces principally from the later 18th and early 19th centuries.

Since 1961 when an American Museum was opened at Claverton Manor, Bath–the only one of its kind outside the United States–it has been possible to see American period rooms on that side of the Atlantic too.

It is worth noting in passing that a number of the illustrations in this book have been taken from the Index of American Design–in itself a not unimportant part of the story. The Index was a Government project undertaken in the 1930s in order to put to work hundreds of unemployed artists and at the same time go some way towards meeting the growing demand for pictorial information on American design and craftsmanship. The crafts and folk arts recorded in watercolours in the Index are those practised by predominantly European immigrants and were selected on the basis of artistic and historic significance. Although work on the Index was terminated shortly after America's entry into World War II in 1941 and has never been resumed, it is probably the largest and most nearly comprehensive record of its kind in the world. An Egyptologist's technique was adopted for the meticulous documentary style of the painting. You will often have to look very carefully at the illustrations to tell which were taken from watercolour originals.

No controls have yet been imposed on the export of this newly discovered national treasure–the furniture, that is: there is not the demand for it that there is for strategic material, for example. The real thrust understandably is in the opposite direction–in bringing the treasure home. And it is intriguing to speculate on just how much still remains to be found and brought back home from the far flung places where adventurous sea captains might have disposed of it. Some good pieces have been found in the West Indies. Others are thought to have been identified in Argentina, and one notable piece–a Salem secretary made about 1800–was found in South Africa some years ago. It now resides with the country's largest collection of American furniture at the former home of the collector himself, Henry Francis du Pont, on a baronial estate in Delaware called Winterthur (pronounced 'Winter-ture') after the Swiss village where Henry Francis's ancestors were born. Other pieces have also been found in Britain and in the Scandinavian countries, but they are thought to have been taken back by returning immigrants or Tory deserters of the new state.

The question of giving names to the periods and styles in American furniture is a tricky one. The term 'early American' has obvious emotional appeal. It is widely used, but very loosely and can be applied to anything from a late 17th-century chest to an early 20th-century radio, particularly by unscrupulous dealers wanting to cash in on the all-pervading interest in Americana. In another sense, however, 'early American' is quite restrictive. It has nothing to do with American Indians, for example, or for that matter with the vast areas of this country first colonized by the Spanish, and it mostly excludes the 19th century, which until quite recently was usually written off as an aesthetic wasteland. It is reserved instead for the products of the original thirteen colonies, which by the early part of the 18th century had come under British rule and which long after independence continued to dominate the whole scene. For all those reasons I am going to try not to use the term 'early American' even though much of the furniture story to be told in this book does in fact take place in the original thirteen colonies.

One of the earliest writers on American furniture, and also one of the earliest collectors, Luke Vincent Lockwood, used the term 'colonial' for the entire period from about 1650 to 1820, apparently choosing to ignore revolution and independence and all that. But then he severely took to task those dealers who advertised the despised products of the 1830s and later as 'colonial'–one man's colonial being, as always, another man's poison.

Properly used, 'colonial' has history on its side, but it gives no indication of the differences that occurred during almost two centuries when it was applicable, and moreover it has too many derogatory overtones to be wholly satisfactory. Consequently, since the furniture styles adopted here were certainly those of the old countries, principally Britain, the least confusing way of describing them is to use the names used over there. Thus, despite some time lags and lingering dissatisfaction over the inadequately American content, most scholars opt for Jacobean, William & Mary, Queen Anne and Chippendale for the styles that flourished here between about 1650 and 1790. After the Chippendale period, however, history triumphs over style, and furniture made in the first thirty-odd years of the new republic is widely referred to as Federal, strong similarities to the work of such English designers as George Hepplewhite and Thomas Sheraton notwithstanding. There is a tendency afoot, though, to call the whole period 'classical' or 'neo-classical' since that's more or less where Hepplewhite and Sheraton got their ideas. But I favour history over style and will consequently stick to Federal, although I am not going to attempt to coin American names for the first four periods.

I am going to venture a suggestion for the remainder of the 19th century, however. Since the term 'millionaire' was coming into circulation in the early part of the century, it might not be a bad idea to extend Mark Twain's 'Gilded Age' to include not just the thirty or so years after the Civil War in the 1860s but also the twenty or so preceding it. I cannot imagine what the

8

6 *The uniquely American writing-arm Windsor. The writing-arm has a shallow drawer underneath it, designed for sand and quills, and a pull-out candlestand; there is another storage box under the seat. Index of American Design.*

7 *A late 18th-century Windsor bench with bamboo turnings. Such turnings are not considered as desirable as the earlier, more vigorous ones.*

8 *Cherry slant-top desk with a compass or star inlay which might have been made in Connecticut or maybe Rhode Island.*

adjectival form would be, but I like it as a name better than the 'Victorian' label which gets attached to most 19th-century happenings wherever they were taking place.

Terminology aside, there is little doubt that something special did take place here in furniture-making, although much work still remains to be done in refining the distinctions between the local product and the imported, not just in stylistic details such as design and decoration but also in construction techniques and the woods used. The early collectors often mixed up British imports with local products, and it is just possible that British dealers who came over looking for bargains in the 1930s might have ended up with American-made Chippendale or what have you, not the British-made variety they thought they were getting! All of which would seem to indicate that there are fewer (or perhaps just more subtle) differences between the two than either detractors or patriots would have us believe. It is not the purpose of this brief survey to enter into the arguments on either side of the debate, but merely to take a look at what has survived and been identified as made in America.

Identifying the various periods is really something of a treasure hunt, starting out with the heavy square-ish shapes of the Jacobean (1650–90), passing through the William & Mary (1690–1720), which seems to be all legs, on to the lighter more graceful curves of the Queen Anne (1720–50), which develops into the more opulent lines and exuberant carving of Chippendale (1750–90) and then back to something lighter and more ethereal in the Federal period (1790–1825) and back yet again into the heavy mix of the middle and late 19th century, from which the 20th century in turn swung away. Along the route there are all sorts of clues, which after you think a minute are mostly self-explanatory despite their anatomical, horticultural, ornithological, geological, mythological, architectural and sundry other guises. The architectural are usually the least self-explanatory, but there will be other clues to help out on those.

There are teardrop pulls and icicle inlays, cabriole legs and sabre legs, scrolled ears, paintbrush feet, comb backs, fan backs, tassel backs, bonnet tops, mushroom finials, pear-shaped pillars, trumpet turnings, inlaid eagles, butterfly supports and snowflakes – or are they stars? – and sunflowers or maybe they're Tudor roses, and tulips and tattered acanthus and anthemion – or is it honeysuckle? or maybe a palm leaf? – and dolphins and swans and lyres and thunderbolts – all scattered here in confusion but really fitting into a specific time and place in the puzzle.

And then there is that vital clue to placing the pieces on the good–better–best scale: proportion. Are the legs of a chair too short for its back, and vice versa? Does the overall width give the chair a squatty appearance, or are height, width and depth in harmony? Does the sewing table have too much leg and too little body and vice versa again? Does the secretary look top heavy? Does the chest of drawers look like a plain old box? And what about the refinements: the turnings, for example, the lathe-work that produced the varying shapes of legs and stretchers and spindles and back-posts and finials on the earliest furniture and on Windsor chairs in particular? Are they bold and masterful, or weak and puny; vigorous or undistinguished, ill-defined and ineptly executed? What about the carving? Was it done by a master, or someone who should have left well alone? Is the apron delicately or clumsily scalloped? Do the ankles sag? Were the back slats and splats finely or carelessly cut? Are they stiff and straight, or slightly curved for greater comfort?

Real *afficionados* in addition like to talk about the patina of old wood – the gloss or shine on 200-year-old mahogany, walnut, cherry and the much-prized figured maples with their tiger-stripes, tight bird's eye whorls and curly wisps and twists – all mysterious defects in nature which lend beauty to a piece of furniture.

If you have trouble identifying those primary woods – even the experts do on occasion – then you're obviously going to baulk somewhat at the thought of secondary woods which are used for the inside works. There is indeed a bewildering variety of such woods. But if you have anything of Sherlock Holmes in you, you will be intrigued to know that proof of American identity is being established under the microscope among the secondary woods. And breathes there a man or woman who wouldn't want to raise the flag when the tiny food cells of a fragment of oak magnified 100 times turn out to be hexagonal rather than round – sure proof of the American red oak as opposed to the light oaks which could be American or European?

Wood analysis as far as furniture goes is a recent and still inexact science, developing as it did out of one man's hobby. That man, Gordon Saltar, began experiments in 1953 with the country's largest collection of American furniture at Winterthur, Delaware. And as a result of Mr Saltar's work, testing thousands upon thousands of minute samples of primary and secondary woods, it is now possible to identify with some certainty, not only the species of wood in a given chair, table, bookcase, but also to relate the species to its geographical habitat. Since many of the trees growing down the east coast of the United States were limited to a specific region and were quite different from those growing in Britain, for example, wood analysis has become a significant tool in underpinning regional differences in style and in separating the old sheep from the goats!

After about 1790 more American woods were being exported inter-regionally and increasingly to Europe, so identification becomes less certain. Some analysis of woods used in European furniture is being done in Europe, but it will be years before a clearer picture emerges of which woods were employed when and where on both sides of the Atlantic.

The final question in any judgment of antique furniture is: can you live with it? and is it comfortable? I recently had to sit on an attractive-looking Windsor chair for about an hour and found the base of the

9 *A New England tilt-top candlestand made of birch with a delicate vase and floral inlay.*

spindles sticking in the base of my spine. When I slithered forward to avoid them I banged my knees on the cross-beams of a handsome 18th-century maple drop-leaf table, which was rather low for the long-legged!

On the whole I have decided that until I can find a charming 19th-century bamboo whatnot that would hold a lot of books, or can afford a rare and elegant music-stand à la Jefferson and an equally rare canterbury to go with it that would hold miscellaneous news-papers and magazines as well as music, I will simply enjoy looking at, rather than living with, American antique furniture.

Intrigued as ever by the occasional furniture from the past, I did once venture rather nervously into the showrooms of a mid-town (that is, central) New York dealer, in search of a late 18th-century sewing table. (Israel Sack, Inc., I later learnt, was one of the first firms in the American furniture business.) I managed to keep my cool when the first piece pointed out to me cost– $8,000 or about £3,200. It was a beautiful elegant little thing with only one drawer and a worn almost threadbare brocade bag underneath. Given the state of my finances I managed to notice that neither it nor those a little cheaper and with more compartments would hold all my dressmaking supplies and equipment. Only a sewing studio would! I think I'll just go on look-ing at all those lovely little pieces from the past.

Good pieces have been known to disappear with their sales records, particularly from the 1920s and 1930s, and there is always the tantalizing possibility of great finds scattered around the world, but on the whole the best pieces from at least the first five periods of American furniture are now known to be in museums or great public or private collections. When they do come on the open market they are only available to the same very wealthy groups–which should come as a surprise to no one.

The most favoured periods, for people with money, that is, used to be Federal and Chippendale, but Queen Anne is top favourite these days, although nothing ever quite equals the incredible prices paid for the uniquely American pieces made during the Chippen-dale period in Philadelphia and Newport, about which more later. All American pieces are not equally de-sirable or high-priced of course, but prices are generally high, so it is not surprising that English dealers get very excited when they think they have an American piece on their hands.

For those with a little less money, there is always the 19th century and the less exalted pieces of the earlier periods. I am told by friends who have done it that it is possible to furnish a home with pieces of considerable charm, usefulness and value, even from the most sought-after Queen Anne period, at less than it would cost to furnish the same home with modern pieces. Those same friends were rather cagey about telling me just how much they had paid for their treasures, how-ever, and I might add that they did have chairs it was not advisable to sit on–restoration lowers the resale value,

13

12

10 *Massachusetts card-table with delicate floral inlay and the much favoured eagle. The sixteen stars over the eagle may not relate to the number of states in the Union at the time the piece was made.*

11 *Recently discovered mahogany desk attributed to John and Thomas Seymour of Boston. Note the vertical sliding tambour doors, delicate checkered stringing around the drawers and top edge and the delightful bell-flowers trickling down the legs.*

12 *Martha Washington armchair from Salem, Massachusetts. This type of chair seems to be peculiar to New England although a somewhat similar chair had been known in old England at an earlier date.*

13 Klismos *type of chairs with sabre legs attributed to Charles Honoré Lannuier of New York. They are grained to simulate walnut with gilt tracery. The carved and gilded lyre splats have eagle's-head terminals. The acanthus carving on the legs is also gilded.*

3

you see, although I have it on the authority of a highly respected dealer that re-gluing the legs on any piece is perfectly acceptable.

For most people it is not enough just to have good, old furniture, perhaps outstanding pieces for their time and type: they want the name of a master craftsman attached to their treasures – and not just any old name. It has to be one of the biggies, sanctified as among the greatest.

But alas for that insistent desire: although many pieces can be assigned with some certainty on the basis of style, construction and wood to a specific period, give or take a few decades, even to a region, give or take a few miles, very few indeed can be traced to their makers.

The names of quite a number of craftsmen are now known – a handful from the late 17th century and many more from the late 18th and the 19th centuries – but
5 very few of them actually signed, labelled or stamped their work. They were not required to do so by the rules of their organizations. Much of the trade was local and the best pieces of any given craftsman were most certainly made for the neighbourhood bigwigs. The only time such pieces would need to be identified was when they had to be sent out for specialized treatment like carving. The pieces that might be more carefully marked, on the other hand, were those that were exported from New England, say, to places in the South and to the West Indies, but they were also likely to be plainer, more standard pieces. After about the middle of the 18th century it became more common for craftsmen to identify their furniture, and as competition grew keener there was an obvious advantage in doing so, but no consistent pattern seems to have been followed even then.

Printed or engraved labels or trade cards were the chief method used for identification, but they were very fragile, easily torn or lost, stained or eaten by insects beyond recognition. A scrawled signature or initials, a brand mark or metal die stamp are only found occasionally. But it is very exciting when any one of them is spotted in hidden and perhaps unsuspected places. A late 18th-century chest of drawers, for example, was once rescued from oblivion in Canada because an alert New York dealer, Mr John Ginsburg of Ginsburg & Levy noticed a label inside it showing the name of a Philadelphia craftsman. The chest turned out to be the first of only four pieces of furniture so far discovered which have the same label, that of Jonathan Gostelowe. Quite recently a handsome high chest of drawers called a highboy was sold at auction as the work of John Goddard and/or John Townsend, two of the very biggest names in Newport, Rhode Island, towards the end of the 18th century. It took up a temporary abode in a New York museum where a curious curator gave it a thorough looking-over and discovered the name of a complete unknown – Benjamin Baker – scribbled in a hidden spot. Now the name might be that of an owner, or it might just be the next big name on the roster of cabinetmaking stars.

Fifty years or so ago no one knew much about Jonathan Gostelowe, William Savery, Benjamin Frothingham, Stephen Badlam, Thomas Affleck or John Seymour, but since a number of fine pieces have been attributed to them with considerable certainty from documentary evidence, many more have been given their name merely by association with the documented pieces.

Nowadays scientific and historical methods are being applied to the realm of antique furniture and a more careful search of the records is going on to support or refute the attribution of any piece to a given maker. Records of ownership are of considerable help in the process, but the "handed down in the family for generations" stories are not usually found to be particularly reliable. Inventories and bills of sale are much more valuable.

Scattered contemporary records show that cabinetmakers were a close-knit bunch and continuously helped each other, so it is not surprising that new names occasionally turn up to prove that many as yet unknown craftsmen worked in ways similar to those of the craftsmen whose names are already on the honours rolls. The delicate process of attribution and often enough re-attribution promises to be endless.

Anyone afraid of fakes certainly should be. Although everything outside a museum is not fake, there is enough that is to make the ignorant and the sophisticated wary. No doubt some people get what they deserve, that hoary old law of supply and demand cranking into operation under pressure for bargains. The rule then is: if you can't trust your dealer, suspect monkey business. A fake is, in fact, sometimes called a 'monkey' in the trade.

Early 19th-century country pieces are thought to have a remarkable resemblance to the very earliest made pieces of the 17th century and are widely advertised under that great misnomer 'early American'. Some of the forms of furniture so advertised, such as dry sinks, had not even been invented in the 17th century.

English antique furniture is actually cheaper here because it is more plentiful and there is less emotional demand for it; so the unscrupulous dealer has another opportunity to cash in on the passion for Americana.

One little trick known to fakers is to add those much wanted signatures and dates. For years one of the earliest chests made here, called a Hadley chest, was thought to be the earliest signed piece of American furniture in existence. A charming authentic-looking inscription read: 'Mary Allyns Chistt – Cutte and Joyned by Nich: Disbrowe'. Nicholas Disbrowe was a known joiner and the chest might well have belonged to Mary Allyn. The initials 'M A' were worked into the patterns on the front panels of the chest. But then it was discovered that Disbrowe was illiterate and a closer examination of the script revealed that the S's lacked serifs – additional proof that the inscription had been written considerably later than the 17th century. The chest itself is still considered a genuine 17th-century piece and now resides with the Bayou Bend Collection in Houston, Texas.

In the late 19th century many earlier styles were widely copied and have sometimes been confused with the genuine articles, not necessarily with intent to deceive. A small desk, for example, was presented to the White House some years ago. It was considered by all concerned to be a genuine product of late 18th-century Baltimore. But it turned out to be a very good example of a late 19th-century reproduction. An inlaid mahogany breakfront bookcase was catalogued for auction in New York recently as the work of Boston craftsmen John Seymour and/or his son Thomas, but it too was subsequently pronounced a late 19th-century copy. It was bought for $8,000 or approximately £3,200. At that price you should really know what you are getting.

Copies or reproductions form a large part of present-day furniture manufacture although, as far as is known, no one is reproducing 19th-century pieces—yet. Plastics are even being used to reproduce the most ornate japanned highboys among other pieces at less than the cost of a copy in wood, let alone of the original piece. But they should fool nobody and are not intended to. There are also widespread imitations of the finest (and sometimes also of the worst) modern designs, such as the Barcelona chair, but such copies are doing no more than following a trend.

By far the most dangerous kind of fake, since few can possibly be built up from scratch, is the rearrangement, the unholy union (or divorce, come to that) of the various parts that make up a piece of furniture—the chest of drawers that doesn't quite match the chest it is sitting on, the bookcase top that doesn't quite fit the desk beneath it, the lowboy or side table that seems to lack a top. Those are some of the things the trained eye is on the look out for, but the real tests lie in the construction. A basic explorer's kit consisting of a tape-measure, magnifying glass, magnet and torch, is usually recommended for those wishing to investigate that realm, but you really have to know what to measure, where to probe and what to magnetize, and all those secrets are, I'm afraid, beyond the scope of this book. But you might ponder on the fact that our friend Jonathan Gostelowe, the late 18th-century Philadelphia craftsman mentioned above, is supposed to be the only cabinetmaker working in that town at that time who placed small shaped support blocks, varying in number from three to eleven, along the front edge of his drawers. That's the sort of information you need in order to make use of the scientific tools of the trade.

14 *The Barcelona lounge chair first designed by Mies van der Rohe in 1929, now manufactured by Knoll International, the company van der Rohe formed in 1945 in collaboration with Hans and Florence Knoll.*

15 *One of the best surviving examples of a great—that is, 'Brewster'–chair. Metropolitan Museum of Art, New York (Gift of Mrs J. Insley Blair, 1951).*

16 *A triple-purpose piece, this bench converts into a table when the back is dropped forward and has a storage box under the seat. Index of American Design.*

17 *Carver chair in the American Museum at Bath.*

18 *A Bible/writing box. This one was owned by a roving sea captain, who, so the story goes, once fell into the hands of pirates.*

15

16

17

18

The Jacobean Period 1650-90

The story of furniture-making in the United States begins with the Pilgrims—the first settlers who came really intending to stay. The earliest period has in fact been called the Pilgrim Century, which has an appealing ring and will no doubt be around for some time, although the other nonconforming Puritan groups that settled the New England states would not have been too happy about being lumped with the Pilgrims. Century, too, is something of an exaggeration. Nothing that has survived can be dated before about the middle of the 17th century. The stylistic term Jacobean is therefore more generally preferred for this period, which runs from approximately 1650 to 1690, because of the affinities with the English style of that name.

Despite the fact that by the 1650s a thin, broken line of European immigrants had settled almost the entire eastern seaboard of North America to varying depths into the interior, American furniture in this earliest period is New England furniture, in fact principally Massachusetts and Connecticut furniture. Whatever good pieces were made in Virginia, Maryland and the Carolinas seem mostly to have disappeared. Many of the earliest adventurers in those parts were not intending to stay. They were looking for gold, and when they found tobacco instead and did stay, they supposedly had none of the traditions of homecraft taken to New England, nor the long cold winter evenings conducive to fireside work!

The first Dutch settlers in the New York area were likewise hoping to make their pile of guilders from the fur trade and get back home. They consequently did not bother too much with domestic comfort here until later in the century.

No documented piece is known to have survived from the first Spanish settlement at St Augustine, Florida. All the furnishings for the present-day restoration there have been imported. Most studies concerned with American furniture do not include any mention of pieces from the areas colonized by the Spanish. Those colonists did not have the variety of furniture forms known to the settlers from northern Europe. The benches, chests and cupboards that have survived from what are now states like New Mexico, Arizona, Colorado and Texas date at the earliest from the mid 18th century but mostly from the 19th century. A New Mexican room with 18th- and 19th-century pieces in it can be seen at the American Museum at Bath.

Meanwhile back in New England the starving years had passed and, as one writer put it, 'the Lord hath been pleased to turn all the wigwams, huts and hovels the English dwelt in at their first coming into orderly, fair and well built houses, well furnished many of them.'

Basic necessities had to be the first order of the day, and no doubt much of the earliest furniture was quite crude. Some handsome pieces have survived, however, which testify to the skill of the early carpenters and joiners, who yet provided the settlers with sturdy utilitarian pieces well suited to their needs. They were mostly made of solid oak, but pine was also commonly used since it was growing abundantly on the doorstep.

Space then as now was at a premium. Wooden chairs and benches or settles, as they were called, had high backs which served a dual purpose: they kept out the draughts as seats and converted into tables when the backs were turned down. The earliest known tables were simply long boards resting on trestles, which were secured with wooden pegs and easily moved out of the way after eating. Later more permanent tables were of the gateleg variety.

16 Stools and forms, now called benches in America, were certainly more common than chairs, which were still something of a luxury even in old Europe. Very few of any of them have survived, but three distinct types of chairs are known, apart from the chair/tables mentioned above. They are the wainscot chair, the Brewster and the Carver chairs, all of which, when they came with arms were referred to in probate records as 'great' chairs. They can look rather throne-like.

19 The name 'wainscot' derives from German/Dutch usage of '*wagenschot*', literally 'waggon board', which referred to the panels of well grained oak used for fine coaches. The chairs themselves have large rectangular or square-ish panels for seats and backs. They have open arms and are sometimes carved in the most magnificent manner over the entire back. No one is absolutely certain whether the very ornately carved ones were locally made or brought over on the *Mayflower*, or more likely some later immigrant ship. It used to be thought that one particularly splendid example

19 *The Hart Room at the Winterthur Museum, Delaware, which houses the country's largest collection of American furniture. The late 17th-century pieces in this room were all made in New England, except for the small gateleg table which is a rare example of New York work at this time. Beyond the wainscot chair on the right is a handsome court cupboard, one of a small group known with a projecting upper section. A Carver chair can be seen by the fireside beyond a joint stool on the left. Henry Francis du Pont Winterthur Museum, Delaware.*

20 *Ornately carved desk box. This type of carving, called Friesian, seems to have done all along the Atlantic coast, but whether inspired by Dutch originals or not remains unknown. Index of American Design.*

21 *A Hadley chest. Such chests were also known as dower or hope chests.*

22 *A press cupboard with a family crest in the centre panel.*

20

21   22

now in the Essex Institute in Salem, Massachusetts, was English; then it was decided that the oak was an American light oak. But recent work in wood analysis seems to indicate that it is impossible to distinguish between the English and American light oaks with any certainty! The cautious consensus is that the less ornately carved wainscots are more likely to have been made on these shores. A plain wainscot chair actually made of walnut was recently established as Virginia work.

Probate records show that cushions were widely used in the average household at this time, so that it was possible to make these rather forbidding-looking seats somewhat more comfortable, although given the long working day and the lack of light it seems doubtful that the Puritans did much sitting around.

The Brewster and Carver chairs are named after two 15, 17 early leaders of the Massachusetts Bay Colony: William Brewster, an elder (1560–1644), and John Carver (1571–1621), the first governor. The Carver is the smaller and less grand of the two, but they were not named in accordance with the position of each man in the hierarchy, merely on the basis of the type of chair they were supposed to bring over with them on the *Mayflower*. This history cannot tell if Carver owned Brewsters or Brewster Carvers!

Both chairs are characterized by the 'turned' spindles, 'turned' on a lathe, that is. The chief difference, apart from that already mentioned, is that the Brewster has double rows of spindles in practically every possible open space–two for the back, two across the front under the seat, and two down the sides, one row above the seat and the other below. The Carver, on the other hand usually has only one row of spindles across the back and that's it for spindles. It is the more common of the two and is known in a variety of sizes, sometimes without arms. Both chairs were widely copied in the late 19th century.

All three types of chair went out of use towards the end of the century, although the spindle chairs are thought to be distant relatives of the Windsor chairs first made in America in the early part of the 18th century and known in abundance from about the middle of the century onwards.

Quite the most decorative pieces in this period are the chests, cupboards and boxes. The latter are usually referred to as Bible, book, desk or writing boxes. But in 18 addition to reading and writing materials, they were probably used to store other valuables and perhaps toilet articles. Probate records reveal that one man kept silver and 'wampon' in his 'desk'. The boxes were 20 in fact the only kind of desk until late in the century. The slanting lids found on some of them probably facilitated reading and writing.

The all-important chest, however, was the essential piece for storage–clothing, linens, blankets, household equipment–and it almost certainly doubled as a bench and probably as a table too. I've sometimes had to use one of my trunks for similar purposes.

Various types of chest are known from the plainest

23

six-board variety to the more decorative panelled and carved ones. But the two types singled out for special attention are the Hadley chest and the Hartford or sunflower and tulip chest, both of which were made along the Connecticut River in Massachusetts and Connecticut. They come with one, two and sometimes three drawers underneath the chest proper—the adolescent stage of a new form, the chest of drawers.

21 The Hadley chest, named after the place in Massachusetts where it was first found, is distinguished by its flat relief carving of flowers and leaves over the entire front—the three-panelled top chest section and the drawer or drawers beneath it. The initials, presumably of the chests' first owners, are invariably woven into the design on the panels. Incised lines usually curl around within the designs and help define it. The chests were mostly painted black, red, various shades of brown and sometimes green, which also helps emphasize the carving and bring out the moulding on drawer fronts. More than 120 Hadley chests are known. One of them, a two-drawer type with a handsome design of tulips, leaves, scrolls and vines worked over the front, carried the fake label mentioned earlier crediting its make to Nicholas Disbrowe.

24 The sunflower and tulip chest on the other hand was mostly found in the Hartford and nearby Wethersfield area of Connecticut. It is characterized by a rather

different kind of decoration. The carving in the three-panelled sections of the front of the chest proper gives it its name. A decorative arrangement of sunflowers appears in the centre panel and stylized tulips in the other two. The sunflowers are variously thought to be asters or even Tudor roses. In addition to the carving, these chests are decorated with variously shaped split spindles, usually painted black and applied to the sections between the panels and on a smaller scale on either side and down the middle of the drawer fronts. Oval turtle-back bosses, also painted black, are planted jewel-like on either side of the black drawer knobs.

Many of the boxes and cupboards have similar carving and decorative motifs, but whilst boxes and chests were in common use, the cupboards were probably only available to the more well-to-do.

There are two types of cupboards—the press and the court. In America the court cupboard has an open shelf either above or below a closed storage section. The press cupboard on the other hand is entirely closed and consists of capacious drawers and shelf sections. The top part of a press cupboard often has splayed sides which open up flat triangular sections used for displaying prized pots or silver. Lots of panelling, some carving and a rare use of contrasting inlay is found decorating the fronts of these cupboards plus the ebonized split spindles and jewel-like bosses mentioned above.

24

23 *The earliest known example of a chest of drawers, dated 1678. Chests, or chests with drawers underneath, were more common at this time. Henry Francis du Pont Winterthur Museum, Delaware.*

24 *A sunflower and tulip chest. Index of American Design.*

Of such basic necessities as beds and cradles very few indeed have survived. It is thought that bed frames were probably quite crude and not considered worthy of preserving, although the probate records indicate that the bed was a prominent piece in most rooms. One or two cradles made of oak or pine panels, reminiscent of the wainscot chairs, are known.

Apocryphal tales abound about who actually made all this early furniture. My favourite is that our friend Disbrowe was once accused of witchcraft in a dispute over a furniture bill. The probate records have revealed that Disbrowe did at least own joiner's tools, which is more that can be said for the two men who were for long considered the country's first furniture craftsmen, John Alden and Kenelm Winslow.

Alden was a young cooper taken aboard the *Mayflower* at Southampton, and Winslow, a later arrival in the Plymouth settlement, was the brother of the Governor, Edward Winslow. The pair of them were credited with some twenty-odd chairs, chests and cupboards found in the Plymouth area, but without the necessary tools among their possessions it seems rather unlikely that they could have made any of them.

Two other men do seem to have had the necessary tools: Thomas Dennis of Ipswich, Massachusetts, and Peter Blin of Wethersfield, Connecticut. Recent studies have shown that it is no longer possible to credit Dennis

with the sixty-odd pieces he once had to his name, but there is some evidence, through pieces that have come down in his family, that he was a skilled maker of wainscot chairs and richly carved chests. Peter Blin, on the other hand is quite a recent discovery and now gets the credit for sunflower and tulip chests once tentatively associated with friend Disbrowe. Poor old Nicholas D. seems to have only one piece still firmly attributed to him – a wainscot chair now owned by the Wesleyan University at Middletown, Connecticut.

The chief makers of the Hadley chests seem to have been a two-family group living in the part of Hadley, Massachusetts, that actually became Hatfield: John Allis and his son Ichabod, and Samuel Belding and his son, Samuel, Jr. But examples of the chest have been found along the Connecticut River from Hartford all the way north to the Vermont border, so other important makers may yet be dug out of the records.

25 *Fall-front cedar secretary from the New York area. This one has heavy bun feet which contrast oddly with the light, rather wispy free-hand painted decoration. The numerous compartments must have made for efficient business. Museum of the City of New York (Gift of Mrs Elon Huntington Hooker).*

26 *A leggy highboy with handsome burl maple veneer from Massachusetts. The legs have trumpet turnings and end in a type of bun foot.*

27 *Early 18th-century daybed. Metropolitan Museum of Art, New York (Gift of Mrs Russell Sage, 1909).*

28 *Walnut desk-on-frame from Pennsylvania. The bail handles on the drawers have replaced the more common teardrop pulls of this period and are harbingers of new things to come.*

25

27

The William & Mary Period 1690-1720

By about 1690 there had been a marked accumulation of wealth among the colonists up and down the eastern seaboard from commerce and piracy and such, just like in the old countries. Log-cabin pioneering was moving west and leaving behind considerable affluence. The furniture of the next thirty-odd years bears witness to the increasing comfort, refinement, luxury even, of the domestic setting.

The best pieces that have survived are no longer just from New England, either. Handsome and quite unique pieces have been found in the New York and neighbouring New Jersey areas, first settled by the Dutch but taken over by the British in the 1660s. The first Quaker and German settlers arrived in William Penn's country, the richly forested land now known appropriately as Pennsylvania, in the 1680s, and their farming and trading soon flourished. Philadelphia sprang into existence as a cultural and trading centre to rival Boston, and good furniture was soon being made in the area. Some pieces have survived from this early period in the area's settlement, but the best were first made in the later Queen Anne period.

Charleston–'Charles Town' in the pre-Revolutionary years–in South Carolina was also developing into a flourishing urban centre, as was Williamsburg, Virginia, but again little seems to have survived from those areas at this time or be known about what kind of furniture was actually made there.

The William & Mary style lasting from about 1690 to 1720/30 is a transitional style, bridging the gap between the massive simplicity of the earliest years and the sophisticated lines of the later 18th century.

It is variously identified by its leggy look, the ball/bun/onion feet and the paintbrush feet, and the drop handles on drawers. These delicious little teardrop pulls, as they are usually called, were almost certainly imported. The Spanish foot is not some undesirable kind of disease, but just another name for the paintbrush foot, which was in fact a Portuguese device!

Oak continued to be used but it was gradually being ousted from favour by such native woods as walnut and maple. These are lighter woods and contributed, with the change in designs, to the less heavy and bulky appearance of the furniture.

Painting and turning – the old lathe-work – remained important parts of decoration, but carving and ebonizing somewhat less so. Inlay had been used occasionally in the Jacobean period and continued to make the odd appearance during this one, but it was usually very simple. Really sophisticated inlay – marquetry, that is – has rarely been found in these parts.

Veneers of considerable beauty, however, were an innovation at this time and were used to decorate drawer fronts on desks and chests, for example. They were cut from those parts of a tree that have particularly attractive figures or grain markings, such as burls. A burl is actually a malformation or wart-like outgrowth thought to have been caused by some kind of injury. Walnut, ash and maple burls have very attractive figures and were used as veneers at this time.

Japanning – an imitation of oriental lacquering – was also introduced into the colonies at this time, but the best of the rare pieces to have survived belong to the next period.

Aside from innovations in decorative techniques the changes that really created the new style were in the shape of things and in the appearance of new forms of furniture.

Considerable refinements can be seen in chairs – always the key form for any changes, since so many of them have survived – and in chests of drawers and tables. The new forms which appear on the scene are the daybed, the upholstered easy armchair with wings, a variety of desks and a dressing table. In addition, peculiar to the New York/New Jersey area, there is the kas (described on page 32), the Dutch equivalent to a cupboard. But what a cupboard!

A chair that had made its appearance earlier but was most widely used in this period is the ladder-back or slat-back with a cane or rush seat. As its name implies, the slat-back, unlike its cousins the Carvers and the Brewsters, has horizontal slats for a back rather than the less comfortable vertical spindles. These slats vary in number from three to as many as six and have a variety of shapes – arched, curved, scooped, indented, pointed, scrolled or winged – and are sometimes graduated from the narrowest at the bottom to the widest at the top. The front and back posts and understretchers continued to be turned. The front posts are sometimes topped with large flattened disks called mushroom finials. The chair itself stayed around for a long time, albeit relegated to country use later in the century. It was effectively revived, mushroom finials and all, by the Shakers in the 19th century (see page 86).

29 *Keeping Room at the American Museum, Bath. A keeping or keepand room was a general living-cum-dining-cum-cooking room.*

Ornately carved chairs with cane seats and backs are known at this time, as are banister-backs and leather upholstered seats and backs, but they are not very common, and there seems to be some uncertainty as to their origin. Banister-back chairs at one New York museum were recently pronounced English!

27 The fancy new material—cane—was sometimes used for the new seat-cum-bed called a daybed, also named a couch in later American usage. (The experts are trying to hold to 'daybed'.) The piece is a sort of extended chair with an adjustable back. It usually has eight legs and is covered with a long thin squab or stuffed cushion. It seems likely that it was more often used as an extra bed rather than for just lounging around. As a form it didn't have a very long life, although some 19th- and 20th-century lounging pieces are probably remote descendants.

32 The big new thing in chairs at this time, however, is the richly upholstered easy chair with a high back and protecting wings, a great improvement in comfort. Its charms were obviously widely recognized, because it stayed around with minor variations well into the 19th century. It is thought that it was initially reserved for the sick and the elderly, and was most often placed in a bedroom. One expert has pointed out that one of the few contemporary portraits showing anyone actually sitting in one is John Singleton Copley's portrait of Mrs John Powell in 1764. And there the painter chose to emphasize the sitter's great age by having her shrunken form lost in the vast depths of an easy chair.

Tables at this time show increasing variety. The gate-leg is still around, but some of them show an interesting variation—butterfly wings instead of gate-leg supports for the extra leaves. These tables in addition have widely raked legs which give them greater stability. Tables with hinged leaves were not unknown in Europe, but the butterflies are a distinctively American development of uncertain direct lineage.

33 A number of medium-sized and small tables show up, too, and were probably used for such leisure activities as reading, writing, playing cards and, luxury of luxuries, having breakfast.

To keep pace with increased letter-writing to and fro across the Atlantic, a deputy postmaster general for North America was appointed in 1692—and new types of desk came on to the scene for more or less the same reason.

The large drop-front type of desk sitting atop two or three drawers was rare in the colonies, but one such piece, marked 'Edward Evans 1707' is the earliest signed and dated piece out of Philadelphia. It resides at Colonial Williamsburg. Much more common were the
25, 28 improvements in the old desk box. First it was put on a frame and given lots of little compartments under the lid. Then it acquired drawers underneath and finally a bookcase on top. All types seem to have appeared as a mysterious new form in the probate records in a wild variety of spellings—schrutoor, screwtor, scrutore, scriptoire—and for some years were inventoried at much higher prices than a common or garden desk,

probably until the novelty or snobbery wore off and the local carpenters started making them. A slant-top desk with a bookcase or other compartmentalized top settled down with the final English form of the word 'secretary'. The piece became much more common later in the century.

Some unsung genius, or perhaps several of them, had gradually realized that the old chests were not very practical—it was not easy getting into them when there happened to be a few objects, human or otherwise, perched on top, and it must have been awfully difficult finding what you set out for in that one big space. Some improvements had already taken place as noted above—drawers under the chest proper and the first chests of drawers. But it must still have been rather back-breaking getting into the bottom drawer which was almost on a level with the floor. The next inspired idea was to put the whole thing on legs. So just as there is a desk-on-a-frame at this point, there is also a chest-of-drawers-on-a-frame. And it was this piece that was to be developed in a unique and exceptional manner in America later in the 18th century, long after it had gone out of fashion in Europe. The piece came to be called a 'highboy' here, nobody knows quite when or how, and the name has a tenacious hold, despite efforts in scholarly circles to get back to the much less colourful names used in the probate records—'high chest' or 'high chest of drawers'.

The highboy's companion, the lowboy, is merely the frame taken out from under the early form of the taller piece, and given drawers and an identity of its own. It is sometimes referred to rather laconically in the records, along with the high chest, as 'and table'. But it soon had a variety of functions—dressing table in the bedroom, side or serving table in the dining room and writing table in the living or drawing room. The term 'lowboy' was actually used in the 18th century, although infrequently, and may have been the inspiration for the newer name of its grander companion. In its later more refined forms the lowboy has a triple-arched skirt with two deep drawers on either side of a shallow one above the higher centre arch of the skirt.

The peculiar contribution to furniture forms made

3

30

31

30 *Walnut lowboy with trumpet turnings and fat teardrop pulls, from Pennsylvania. Collection of Colonel and Mrs Miodrag R. Blagojevich.*

31 *Early 18th-century painted kas from the New York area. Metropolitan Museum of Art, New York (Rogers Fund, 1909).*

32 *An early 18th-century upholstered wing chair, with horizontally rolled arms. The paintbrush feet and vigorously turned stretchers blend in with a new leg shape–the cabriole. Index of American Design.*

33 *Corner of the Murphy Room in the Bayou Bend Collection, Houston Museum of Fine Arts, Texas. The slat-back chair on the right has the flattened disk (so-called 'mushroom') finials on the arms. Small graceful tables like this one were outmoded by the larger space-saving butterfly type.*

by the Dutch settlers in and around New York is the kas–a modification of the original Dutch *kast* (hence the accepted plural form, 'kasten') which being freely translated means a cupboard, but a huge one. It is also sometimes freely translated as wardrobe, but since it usually has shelves inside not hanging space, I am going to stick to cupboard. Red gum, or bilsted as it is called locally, from which the kasten were sometimes made has been identified as a quite common secondary wood in furniture made in the New York/New Jersey area, but its use was not exclusive to that area as used to be thought.

The kas's chief claim to glory lies in the painted decoration found on some of them. That painting is occasionally done *en grisaille*, i.e. in various shades of grey, but others are known with a variety of colours. The entire front and sometimes the sides too are painted in very realistic designs of fruit, birds and flowers–so realistic often you feel you could grasp hold of them. That's the *trompe l'œil* effect–deceiving the eye. These paintings are said to be among the first still-lifes done hereabouts.

Made for quick getaways, the kas is easily dismantled unless it has been incorrectly restored. The overhanging cornice or top lifts off, the doors come out and the sides and back lift off the base which usually consists of two large drawers. When not painted these pieces are decorated with lots of panels and bosses. They continued to be made throughout the 18th century and

into the 19th. Anyone interested in owning one of the later ones might be lucky enough simply to remove it from a suburban New York basement with the owner's blessings–which is how the earliest collectors all operated, except that they removed things from attics! The average New York apartment, however, would be swamped by such a piece, and scarcely has need of it because of generous closet-space–the New York equivalent of built-in or walk-in cupboards.

The work of only one craftsman has been identified with any certainty for this period: John Gaines of Portsmouth, New Hampshire. Gaines is known for some handsome chairs that descended in his family. They display a lively combination of Queen Anne features, such as an elegantly vase-shaped back splat, and William & Mary characteristics, such as paintbrush feet, block-and-vase-turned legs, and bulbous turned stretchers. Recent research has revealed that Gaines' father John senior and brother Thomas, both of whom lived in Ipswich, Massachusetts, also turned their hands to furniture-making among their numerous other activities. The delicate process of attributing chairs to Gaines senior is now going on with a little help from the numerous entries for chairs in his account book, now in the Winterthur library. Others may yet be assigned to Thomas.

34 *A rare early sofa made in Pennsylvania. The cabriole legs have trifid feet and the rear legs are of the rounded stump-like variety that became a characteristic of Philadelphia work. Metropolitan Museum of Art, New York (Rogers Fund 1925).*

35 *Walnut desk-on-frame made in New England.*

36 *Early mahogany tea-table probably made in Pennsylvania or neighbouring New Jersey about 1750. The cabriole legs end in panelled web feet. The scalloped corners of the table were possibly designed for candleholders. Tea-drinking became quite general in the 1740s, and much of the social life of the colonies revolved around the tea-table thereafter.*

34   35

The Queen Anne Period 1720-50

By 1720, of course, good Queen Anne had been dead for some years. The furniture style that bears her name, however, flourished in the colonies from about that time until about 1750/60, and in fact the simple graceful lines of the style lingered on for most of the rest of the century, particularly in country furniture.

During this period Philadelphia comes into its own as a cultural and trading centre, and a taste for worldly things including fine furniture makes steady headway in that Quaker city and even in Puritan Boston, of which a writer of the day said: 'a gentleman from *London* could almost think himself at home in *Boston*, when he observes the numbers of the People, their Houses, their Furniture, their Tables and their Dress and Conversation, which is as splendid and showy, as that of the most considerable Tradesman in *London*.'

Considerable tradesmen in Newport, New York and Charleston were not far behind the pace-setters in Philadelphia and Boston, although as has oft been repeated in these pages, much still remains to be learned about furniture craft south of Philadelphia.

The seaports along the east coast were doing very well indeed, though. In fact the active trade between the colonies up and down that coast–furniture made in the North, for example, exchanged for food grown more easily in the South–was laying the foundation for later political unity, a fact that did not go unnoticed by HM Commissioners, who in 1733 reported: 'the People of New England, being obliged to apply themselves to manufactures more than others of the Plantations who have Benefit of a better soil and warmer Climate [have made] such improvements . . . lately . . . in all sorts of Mechanic Arts, that not only Scrutores, Chairs and other Wooden Manufactures, but Hoes, axes and other Iron utensils are now exported . . . to the other Plantations, which if not prevented may be of ill consequence to the Trade and Manufacture of this Kingdom, which Evil may be worthy of the consideration of a British Parliament.'

36

American craftsmen at this time as earlier had only the simplest tools of the cabinetmaker's craft, and although the latest ideas in design and construction were constantly being brought over by new immigrants, there were no reference books for checking out details. Even the pattern books that began coming over in the second half of the century were not always accurate on construction. Imported pieces did act as models, but the craftsmen were essentially on their own. That even simple furniture at this time has fine rhythmic lines and well balanced composition makes their achievement all the more notable.

Recent research has shown, moreover, that certain distinctive regional characteristics began to make their appearance about this time. Distinctive work had long ago appeared along the Connecticut River valley through what is now the states of Connecticut and Massachusetts, as noted earlier, and Connecticut craftsmen continued to hew their own line in materials and styles for the next 100 years or more. It is perhaps not so surprising that differences in line and decoration have been noted in the work of various parts of New England when you consider how tenaciously the early settlers stuck to their own ideas and formed splinter groups to go off into the wilderness and set up their own communities whenever they didn't agree with some aspect of the rules laid down by the local hierarchy. In addition Dutch, Swiss, French and German immigrants, and those from all parts of the British Isles, all made their special contributions to the regional aspects of American furniture.

37 Philadelphia work is not quite like New England's. The former is richer and more expansive, whereas the latter goes in for leaner proportions and plainer surfaces. New York, understandably enough, lies stylistically as well as geographically somewhere in between. Its day as top dog did not arrive until the end of the century. From what little is known about work in Virginia and the Carolinas, it seems that a somewhat plain style was fashionable in those parts.

Furniture had begun to flow and curve in the preceeding period, but this is when the curve really takes over, and one of the hallmarks of the style is the sinewy

34 line of the cabriole leg, an ancient form based on an animal's leg from the knee down. It appears on just about every piece–chairs of every sort, desks, secretaries, highboys, lowboys, tables. The name 'cabriole' derives from an Italian word via the French. The former had the sense of a goat leaping (Latin for goat = *caper*), and the latter of a horse lashing out with a kick. One expert has pointed out a notable springiness in the furniture of the period largely as a result of the cabriole legs. It is a springiness that was occasionally mocked by painter/satirist William Hogarth in England. You

37 *Vauxhall Dining Room at the Winterthur Museum. The chairs and highboy in the background were made in Philadelphia, but the table was more probably made in Virginia, which makes it quite rare. Henry Francis du Pont Winterthur Museum, Delaware.*

have to watch out for the really bandy ones and for the sagging ankles!

The feet on the cabriole legs are mostly of the pad or Dutch variety, small, roundish and flattish as the first name implies, and sometimes raised from the floor by disc-shaped cushions. There are numerous variations on this foot as well as names for them, but the principal ones are 'slipper' with a pointed toe, 'webbed' like a duck's foot, or more deeply cut into the 'trifid' or three-cleft shape. The claw-and-ball foot also makes its first appearance late in this period, especially on New York furniture. That device is thought to have been derived from an ancient Chinese symbol for evil—a dragon grasping a pearl.

Carving begins to supersede turning, except on Windsor chairs about which more later, as the chief decorative technique; but it was used sparingly at this point, primarily on cabriole knees and at the centre of a chair's crest rail, for example.

43   Japanning as a decorative technique was advertised in Boston in the early years of the 18th century along with such other inducements to the curious as experiments in electricity. The former has not weathered the years as well as the latter, unfortunately. A simplified version of the European imitation of oriental lacquerwork, japanning was something of a passing fad in the colonies and its popularity was on the wane by mid century when figured woods and carved ornament became the latest thing. Few pieces have survived from those early experiments, and those that did have seriously deteriorated. The raised figures—whimsical animals, flowers, people, birds—that form part of the design on the best japanned pieces were built up in layers of whiting and varnished over, and have, alas, begun to crack and crumble. But some of their charm is still visible. It is thought that one set of Queen Anne chairs were actually sent to China later in the century for their oriental lacquer decoration. In this late 20th century it has become possible to make a facsimile of japanning in plastics, wouldn't you know!

My favourite teardrop pulls disappear and are replaced by small bail handles which look a bit like shallow boats with stem and stern more or less vertical. They were probably much easier to get hold of. Simple escutcheon plates in the shape of butterflies or bats formed the backing to the handles and were destined to grow grander and more flamboyant by the decade. All the hardware continued to be imported, though, until well into the 19th century and little is yet known about local manufacture in that area.

The principal wood used in this period is black walnut, found in abundance all along the eastern seaboard. Butternut or white walnut was often used in country pieces. Maple was also popular, particularly in New England and Pennsylvania, and cherry in New York and Connecticut. Mahogany was being imported into Charleston, Philadelphia and New England by this time, but very few examples of mahogany furniture are found until the Chippendale period when it becomes the dominant wood.

38 *Lowboy of cherry, probably made in Connecticut about 1740. (There exists a matching highboy.) Note the bail handles, the bat-like escutcheon plates behind them and the cabriole legs with pad feet. The acorn pendants are all that remain of the extra legs seen on the earlier highboy [26].*

39 *Mahogany cellaret—a rare Southern piece of about 1760. Index of American Design.*

40 *Japanned looking-glass thought to have been made in the New York area about 1740.*

40

41 *The Perley Parlour of about 1763 at the American Museum, Bath.*

42 *Comb-back Windsor armchair probably from the Pennsylvania area. Index of American Design.*

43 *Japanned highboy made in Boston about 1745. The japanning was probably done by Thomas Johnston (or Johnson) who is perhaps the best-known of only a handful of men practising the art in the colonies at this time. Henry Francis du Pont Winterthur Museum, Delaware.*

42

41

40

34 Except for the appearance of the sofa and the folding top card table, there was little that was new in the way of furniture forms at this point, although most of the older forms were considerably changed and refined. The scale is more domestic but the appearance is singularly urbane.

2 There are marked changes in chairs as always. The centre back now consists of a single vertical splat which has a vase-like shape and is sometimes said to echo that of Chinese porcelains. Curving stiles either side of the centre splat and a curving crest rail complete the framework of the back. The centre of the crest rail is often finely carved, with shell motifs for example, as are the knees of the cabriole legs. The cabriole legs gave strength and support to the width and made structural underbracing in the form of stretchers unnecessary, but the latter are often retained, particularly in New England where the legs tend to be more slender.

The daybed and the easy chair were still around with the appropriate leg changes to cabriole, but the former was gradually ousted from favour by the appearance of the sofa, one or two of which are found at this time, and by the fact that larger houses made extra bedrooms possible.

35 Desks continue the logical lines of development mentioned in the previous period. The desk-on-a-frame rapidly became something of an anachronism, but the slant-top desk with drawers underneath was due for a long life, as was the secretary with the case top. Both were tried with puny little cabriole legs but they were replaced by more solid brackets. The secretaries have another refinement–a broken scrolled pediment, called a bonnet top.

The highboy continues on its merry way upwards, now to be crowned with the same bonnet top as the secretary, although it retains cabriole legs, long slender ones, and now has all the characteristics–give or take a few details–and all its uniquely American appearance that it was to retain for most of the rest of the century.

A few high post beds–four-posters in the vernacular–are known at this time with cabriole legs, tester or canopy and draperies, but they were not made in quantity until after about 1751.

40 Looking-glasses–the term 'mirror' seems not to have been introduced before about the end of the 18th century–are also thought to have been made locally at around this time or even a little earlier, although there is much dispute going on at the present time as to the English or American origin of surviving examples. The plate glass was almost certainly imported, so the argument hinges on who made the frames. They are usually rectangular with a decorative top and maybe bottom with a few scrolls down the sides. They were popular pieces for the japanner's art. Cautious consensus again hovers around the theory that the plainer frames are the ones most likely to have been made here.

Very little is known about individual craftsmen at this time–which must be very frustrating for those who

44 *New England Windsor armchair.*

need to have a big name attached to their treasures, and particularly now that the period is fashionable.

John Gaines continued to work in Portsmouth, New Hampshire, until his death in 1743, but no pieces can yet be attributed to him in the purely Queen Anne style.

Some early work of three big names in the Chippendale period is known, however, and it is possible that further research will make revelations in that direction. The three men concerned are William Savery of Philadelphia, and John Goddard and Job Townsend of Newport. Several labelled Savery pieces are known–a daybed, side chairs and an armchair and one labelled Townsend secretary. A lowboy is attributed to Goddard because it has some unusual characteristics, such as undercut talons on the claw-and-ball foot, which are associated with his later work. Other new names are emerging from a careful search of the records, but no new attributions can be made with any certainty. Thomas Elfe was known to be active in Charleston before 1747, but all the pieces now attributed to him again belong to the later Chippendale period.

Painted chests, some with drawers, and really survivals of a much earlier form, are attributed to Robert Crosman of Taunton, Massachusetts. The definitive article on Crosman is called 'The Tantalizing Chests of Taunton'. By 1739 Crosman was advertising himself as a drum-maker, and although he lived to the ripe old age

of 92 he doesn't seem to have made any other furniture.

It is thought that the Windsor chair first made its appearance on this side of the Atlantic in the late 1720s in the Philadelphia area, and that it was in fact known as a Philadelphia chair for some time. Not many have survived from this early period, however, but there is widespread evidence of its popularity even in sophisticated circles from about the middle of the century onwards, after which time distinctive Pennsylvania and New England versions are found.

The earliest Windsors here have low rounded backs, but subsequent upward developments gave them much more dash and elegance. Many varieties of backs are known but six principal ones are usually singled out: low-back, comb-back, fan-back, hoop-back, New England armchair and loop-back. The best ones have a saddle seat shaped for more comfortable sitting. As you might expect for such a prolific form, names for similar types vary somewhat. Elegant settees also come Windsor style.

Windsors were almost certainly first made for outdoor use and painted against the weather – 'green like those in the gardens of France', as one visitor noted, but other colours were used. Benjamin Franklin had two dozen painted white. Thomas Jefferson ordered four dozen in black and gold.

One particular form, the writing-arm Windsor, is peculiarly American, and self-explanatory. Jefferson

45 *The Commons Room at Winterthur Museum. The earliest Windsors were low-backs, two of which can be seen on either side of the small table in the centre. The bow-back is merely a low-back with a curving addition to the centre back. Two loop-backs with bamboo turnings are seen on either side of the table at the left. Henry Francis du Pont Winterthur Museum, Delaware.*

developed a variation of this type so that the seat revolved. A writing-arm that had belonged to Ward Beecher, father of Harriet Beecher Stowe of *Uncle Tom's Cabin* fame, was recently sold at auction for $3,200 or approximately £1,280.

Windsor chairs hold a special place in American affections of course because the revolutionaries who met to plot and plan in Philadelphia in the 1770s sat around in handsome Windsor chairs. Many are now preserved in that city's Independence Hall, although it seems that only one of the original ones used there has so far come to light.

The Chippendale Period 1750-90

By the 1760s the independent-minded colonists were not at all happy about the restrictions being imposed on their trade and manufactures by the British, and friction with Westminster was on the increase.

The scions of wealthy families doing the Grand Tour of Europe were counselled against purchasing furniture in England, because 'In the humour people are in here, a man is in danger of becoming invidiously distinguished who buys anything in England which our Tradesmen can furnish.' And as the same correspondent emphasized, 'Household goods may be had as cheap and as well made [here] from English patterns.' The lavishness of the furnishings of one Manhattan mansion had even been cited in the British Parliament in 1759 as a reason for increasing colonial taxes!

Liberty songs were being sung in many corners of the thirteen colonies and in 1773 there was that furious dumping of tea in Boston harbour. The widespread sympathy felt for that rebellious act was given vent in such ditties as *A Lady's Adieu to her Tea-Table* which was widely circulated in the newspapers of the day and went in part as follows:

No more shall my teapot so generous be
In filling the cups with this pernicious tea,
For I'll fill it with water and drink out the same,
Before I'll lose LIBERTY that dearest name,
Because I am taught (and believe it is fact)
That our ruin is aimed at in a late act,
Of imposing a duty on all foreign Teas,
Which detestable stuff we can quit when we please.
LIBERTY'S the Goddess that I do adore,
And I'll maintain her right until her last hour,
Before she shall part I will die in the cause,
For I'll never be govern'd by tyranny's laws.

46 *The Deming Parlour of 1770–80 at the American Museum, Bath.*

All the unrest culminated in the Declaration of Independence and seven years of war from 1776 to 1783. But it did not impede the introduction of the latest furniture styles from England, which more or less coincided with the appearance on this side of the 1762 and subsequent editions of Thomas Chippendale's *Gentleman and Cabinet-maker's Director*.

Philadelphia was by this time the undisputed centre of furniture-making among other things, with Newport, Rhode Island, running a close second. The latter was also a Quaker stronghold but was no more deterred thereby from a taste for worldly elegance. The influence of both cities was strongly felt in the areas all around them, but regional distinctions continue to be made for work done in New York, the Boston/Salem area and Connecticut. A new urban school makes a strong showing at this time in Charleston, South Carolina.

It used to be thought that much if not most of the furniture used in Virginia and the South had been imported, either from the North or from Britain, and that much if not most of it had been destroyed during the Civil War in the 1860s. Recent research however indicates that probably quite large quantities of furniture were made in those parts by itinerant craftsmen and skilled slaves. More than one complaint by white migrant joiners has survived against the preference in the area for cheap Negro labour. But much still remains to be learned about the work of both groups. Some distinctive work has recently been noted from Maryland and Kentucky for this period, but who should get the credit for it is still very vague.

The stylistic changes are really culminations of earlier developments and there are few new forms to report. A large bookcase called a 'breakfront' because of a projecting centre section makes a rare appearance on the American scene, and there are some new kinds of small table. Chests and secretaries get kneehole sections, and the chest-on-a-chest becomes a showpiece.

The chief characteristic of the period lies in the sophisticated carving, usually identified by its Rococo exuberance. The term 'Rococo' describes the endless variations in animal, plant and mineral forms which appear in the carved designs on numerous pieces, often in an asymmetrical manner and inspired by Chinese designs. The Oxford dictionary says the word is a fanciful formation on the stem of the French word '*rocaille*', first used to describe elaborate ornament consisting of rocks and pebbles and sea-shells and leafy scrolls. But it has been suggested that it might also be a contraction of the two French words '*rocaille*' and '*coquille*', the latter ('shell'), being one of the principal motifs in the designs. It often has a derogatory sense in English and American, come to that. Thomas Jefferson called it 'that burden of barbarous ornament'. It is nevertheless used with elegance and to considerable effect at this time particularly in Philadelphia work.

The cabriole leg continues to play an important role, but it now almost always has a claw-and-ball foot. Various regional differences have been noted in the

47

47 *A closed bonnet-top mahogany highboy from Newport. This piece has many of the characteristics long associated with the Goddard/Townsend group of craftsmen, including the undercut talons clearly visible on the front feet. But the signature of a completely unknown craftsman was recently found inside it–Benjamin Baker–which seems to indicate that the G/T group had skilled competitors.*

48 *Interlaced ribbon-back on Massachusetts open armchair, which once belonged to Salem merchant-prince Elias Hasket Derby. The swept-back side claws on the feet are typical of Massachusetts work.*

49 *Philadelphia tassel-back chairs.*

handling of that foot. In Newport, for example, the claws are undercut and in Massachusetts the two side 47 talons are swept back. In Philadelphia work again the 48 hollows above the claws are particularly well defined. In New York work the whole foot has a rather square and angular appearance. The scroll foot—rather like toes turned up and over—and the hairy paw foot are extremely rare on American furniture at this time.

Plain rounded stump-like rear legs are mostly a feature of Philadelphia chairs, whereas tapering rear 49 legs broadening at the lower ends are found on many New York chairs. One reason that has been offered for the Philadelphia stumps is that they were left deliberately plain because only the servants saw them!

Straight legs are also found on chairs, tables and sofas, for example, and such legs occasionally have a blocked Marlborough foot. No one seems to know how 54 that name was assigned. For the time being it is principally associated with the work of Thomas Affleck of Philadelphia, where all straight-legged furniture with or without the block foot was apparently given the Marlborough label.

The piercing or decorative cutting of the central splat and the development of a serpentine or cross-bow shaped crest rail are the two most important developments in chairs. The designs and carving used for the centre splat show endless variations and combinations. Pierced horizontal rungs or ladder-backs are also found 52 —sophisticated relatives of the earlier slat-backs which were still around in country use.

Chairs from Newburyport, Salem, Boston and Roxbury, sometimes called the Massachusetts Bay Group, continue to have an overall lightness in their proportions, which perhaps accounts for the persistence of stretchers to reinforce the understructure. New York chairs are noted for their wide seats and more generous proportions. Philadelphia chairs rival the New England products for their elegance and graceful proportions and are usually more ornately carved.

But the great glory of Philadelphia cabinetmaking at this time is the final triumphant form of the highboy, 63 already seen rising to great heights in the Queen Anne period. Ironically enough, having solved the bending problem of long ago, in this their final form, often seven to eight feet tall and 'nearly as high as the ceiling' as one contemporary put it, they created the reverse problem. Access to the top drawers now called for step ladders!

Practicality aside, these magnificent highboys are the real showpieces of late 18th-century American craftsmanship, and ever since the first big sale of American pieces, the Howard Reifsnyder collection, in 1929, they have been among the highest priced. It was at that sale that one such piece went to Henry Francis du Pont for the startling sum of $44,000—more than £17,500—after he had successfully beaten off a challenge from none other than press lord William Randolph Hearst.

After the rich colouring and exotic lustre of the imported mahogany, of which most Philadelphia high-

48

boys are made, has had its effect, the first eyecatcher on these pieces is the broken pediment or top. It comprises scrolled swans' necks rising over a lattice or carved area on either side of a centre finial—a torch, a flower-filled urn or vase, or something that looks like a peanut jewel in a pierced and leafy setting. Matching finials on a smaller scale occasionally crown the front corners. Flower garlands will sometimes trail down the slender quarter colonettes which flank the drawers on both the upper and lower sections and bring the eye to rest on the carving of the skirt and knees and on the decorative panel often found at the centre of the bottom drawer. There, among other designs, will be found those based on the fables of La Fontaine or Aesop, depending on how far back you like to go for sources.

Equally lustrous in their use of imported mahogany are the highboys made in Newport. But these pieces are usually more restrained in their decoration, relying simply on a handsome shell in the centre of the skirt and on panelling carried up into the scrolled pediment. The cabriole legs on Newport highboys are often longer and slimmer, too, and a closed bonnet top is favoured with only a centre finial. One such piece brought over $100,000, or about £40,000, at a recent auction. That was the piece mentioned earlier (page 16) on which the scribbled signature of an unknown maker was found.

Other woods such as cherry and maple were used for

50 *Patuxent Bedroom at the Winterthur Museum. The bed, tea-table and lowboy are considered Pennsylvanian work, but the chairs may have been made in Maryland. Henry Francis du Pont Winterthur Museum, Delaware.*

51 *The Samuel Powel Drawing Room at the Metropolitan Museum of Art in New York. Powel was mayor of Philadelphia during the memorable decade 1770–80 when the American colonies established their independence. In 1765, whilst on the Grand Tour of Europe, he was counselled by his uncle against buying furniture or any other household goods in England because of the intense local dissatisfaction with Westminster's policies towards the colonies at the time. Most of the furniture in the room is the work of Philadelphia craftsmen.*

highboys, particularly in Connecticut and Massachusetts. Very few such pieces are known from New York and none at all from Virginia or the Carolinas. The woods and decorations of the lowboy basically matched those of its grander companion.

Whilst the Philadelphians were indulging their fancies in wonderfully carved frills and fripperies, something quite different but equally special and uniquely American was going on in Newport. There the hallmark of the period is the block front or 'sweld' front as described by one of its best-known craftsmen, 55 John Goddard. On slant-top desks and secretaries, where it is seen to best advantage, the blocking usually consists of three flat raised sections with slightly rounded ends separated by narrow concave sections. In the work of the Goddard family and their relatives in the Townsend family, the blocking is usually crowned with magnificently carved shells either raised in relief or incised and called 'intaglio'.

Blockfront furniture was also made in Massachu-64 setts, New York and Connecticut, but only in the latter state does it seem to have been successfully combined with the shell carving associated with Newport work.

Handsome secretaries and desks are found at this time without the block-and-shell design, and rare 53 examples are known with a *bombé* or kettle-shaped base. For the time being, the latter are only associated with the name of John Cogswell and Boston workmanship.

Another tall piece, much in evidence at this time and 56, 62 also something of a showpiece, is the chest-on-chest or double chest as it is variously called. It was apparently known earlier, but no examples have survived that can be dated before about 1760–80. By the end of the century it had become something of an anachronism, though at least two examples are known which belong chronologically to the next period but stylistically to this, and both happen to be magnificent examples of the form. They are now part of the collections at Yale University and the Boston Museum of Fine Arts.

Both pieces used to be attributed to Samuel McIntire of Salem, Massachusetts, or at least the carving was thought to be his work. McIntire is one of the big names in the Federal period. He is now credited with the carving on only one of them, 'the masterpiece of Salem' in the Boston museum. On the other piece, at Yale, there is a well-known label carrying these instructions: 'Keep this side up & preserve it from the Sun, from Wet & from bruises. It is of consequence enough to merit great attention.' Careful examination of the handwriting some years ago revealed it to be identical with that of Stephen Badlam, a relatively unknown craftsman, but with that discovery now ranked among the best.

Large dining tables are very scarce indeed from this period, although the drop-leaf type is known to have been around both in the oval form and in a newer square shape. Numerous smaller, more specialized tables have survived, however, some with the drop-leaf form. The 60 Pembroke or breakfast is one of the latter, although it reverses the usual order in having the centre section 57 wider than the leaves. The folding-top card table with

52 *Massachusetts ladder-back chair.*

53 *Mahogany secretary with* bombé *or kettle-shaped base. It is thought that the* bombé *base was only attempted in Boston.*

54 *The frame of a mahogany four-poster with Marlborough block feet attributed to the Goddard/Townsend group of craftsmen in Newport.*

55 *Pride of Newport. This block and shell carved mahogany desk is a rare example of a labelled piece by John Townsend (1732–1809) long thought to be one of the key figures in the Goddard/Townsend group of craftsmen.*

56 *Mahogany chest-on-chest attributed to Thomas Affleck. This piece is known to have survived a burning house in Germantown, just outside Philadelphia, at the time of the Revolutionary War. It is presently on display at the State Department in Washington.*

53

54

55

56

51

57 *New York games table with an inlaid chess and
backgammon board. The gadrooning along the skirt edge, the
chunky claw-and-ball feet and the extra leg are all
considered New York characteristics. Index of American
Design.*

58 *Mahogany lowboy attributed to William Savery of Philadelphia. Index of American Design.*

a gateleg or swivel form is quite common, but the most
61 characteristic small table is the tripod tea-table or candlestand with a bird-cage support for tilting and turning. A piecrust edge is usually associated with Philadelphia work and an elongated leaf-carved vase pedestal is noticed on Charleston work. A rectangular side table called a pier table, which often has a marble top, became an almost indispensable dining room piece, the forerunner of the sideboard. 'Pier' is an architectural term for the section of a wall between two windows, which is where this type of table stood.

Apart from the sophisticated pieces made in the fashionable and wealthy seaports, many less ornate country pieces have survived from this latter part of the 18th century. Mostly made of readily available local woods like cherry, maple, pine, red or sweet gum, and tulip-poplar, rather than the expensive imported mahogany of their haughty sisters, they are often well proportioned and have considerable charm. Some of the
59 corner cupboards, much sought-after today, are particularly attractive. The tulip tree (*Liriodendron tulipifera*)–it has yellow and orange tulip-shaped flowers in May or June–used to be called 'canoewood' because the Indians made dugout canoes from it. It was long a favourite secondary wood in practically all regions, and its presence is considered a reliable sign of American identity.

Sawbuck tables–a sort of trestle with x-shaped end supports linked by a horizontal cross beam, a common sight on picnic grounds here–are an obvious 20th-century remembrance of a common country type.

The most interesting of the country furniture at this time, with a special character of its own, is that of the German and Swiss settlers in Pennsylvania–the term 'Pennsylvania Dutch' is a corruption of *Deutsch*, meaning German. The first such settlers arrived from the Rhineland late in the 17th century at the invitation of William Penn himself. They brought with them a colourful tradition in the decorative arts which they carried on down into the 19th century.

Among the pieces essential to country housekeeping, aside from tables, chairs and beds, were a *schrank* or
66 cupboard, not unlike the Dutch kas, and a dower chest. The latter is the most decorative of the common household pieces in the Pennsylvania German communities. Just such a form inspired the makers of the Hadley chest in 17th-century Massachusetts (page 24).

In this case, however, the chests are long and rectangular with at most two drawers side by side across the length of the bottom. The fronts and sometimes the top and sides as well are painted, usually in panels with a variety of such traditional motifs as unicorns, hearts, tulips, cherub heads and horsemen woven together within leafy, floral or geometrical borders. An occasional moral directive like 'Better to be dead than faithless' will be found worked into the design along with the owner's name or initials and the date in Roman characters. Many of the most attractive of these chests were made by Christian Selzer of Jonestown, Dauphin County, in central Pennsylvania.

The work of some twenty-five craftsmen in high style Chippendale has been identified with some certainty but, as has often been repeated in these pages, more pieces have been attributed to five or six of them than can be justified by documentary evidence. Some 100 craftsmen are known to have been working in the Philadelphia area alone at this time, yet frustratingly little has been discovered about the makers of the beautiful highboys. Any or all of the holy trinity made up of Thomas Affleck, Benjamin Randolph and William Savery may have made these pieces, but so may many another whose history, advertisements or other business cards and records have not survived or have not yet come to light.

Top of the list not just alphabetically, Thomas Affleck is considered by many experts to have produced 6 some of the best Philadelphia Chippendale furniture. He is known to have worked for Governor John Penn and other local notables, and his work is usually distinguished by its elaborate carving and the use of straight, so-called Marlborough legs with or without blocked or plinth-like feet. He immigrated to Philadelphia in 1763 when he was about 23 from his native Scotland, probably via some training in London. In 1777 he was banished to faraway Virginia for his Royalist sympathies; but in 1783 he was back in town and, if his occupational tax rate is anything to go by, his business was booming. His tax for that year was considerably higher than that of any of his contemporaries.

Benjamin Randolph, born in New Jersey, is most famous for his chairs and for an elaborate business card, which reproduces designs from Chippendale's *Director*. The chairs that are the principal reason for his fame descended in his wife's family. All but one in the group of five side chairs and one armchair are elaborately carved in the advanced Rococo manner with acanthus leaves trailing over the cabriole knees, leafy floral chains trickling down the stiles and across the crest rail and over the intricately cut centre splat. They are known as 'sample chairs', because it is thought that they must have been made to show off the cabinetmaker's skill. Once thought to be English-made, they have been pronounced American on the basis of the construction. The wing chair from the set brought $33,000, or over £13,000, at the 1929 Reifsnyder sale mentioned earlier. Randolph is also known to have worked for Thomas Jefferson.

William Savery became a big name after a handsome 5 lowboy carrying his label was spotted in the Van Cortlandt House Museum on the outskirts of New York a number of years ago. Some twenty labelled pieces have subsequently come to light, and for some years almost anything of artistic worth was attributed to him. The inventory of his estate at death made no mention of carving tools, so either someone did the carving for him–a common enough practice–or his work was plainer than has been thought. For that reason, it does not seem possible to credit him with highboys, the grander ones at any rate.

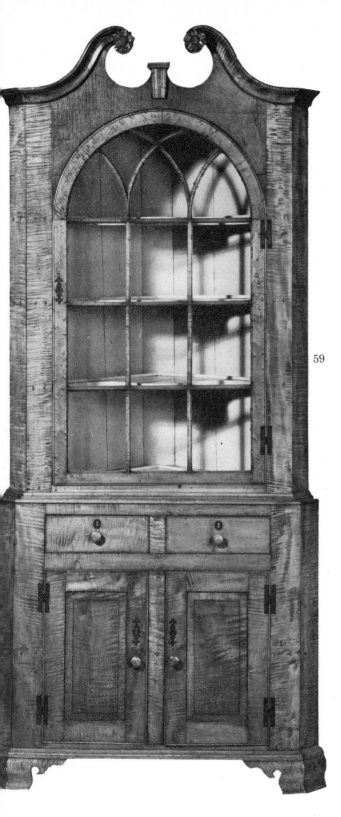

59 60

61

59 *Late 18th-century curly maple corner cupboard from Pennsylvania. Such pieces were popular in most homes, either built into the wall or free-standing, and are great favourites with antique collectors today.*

60 *Late 18th-century mahogany Pembroke table from Philadelphia.*

61 *Late 18th-century mahogany tripod table from New York. The top, with its piecrust edge, revolves and tilts into a vertical position on the bird-cage support.*

The known work of Jonathan Gostelowe is unusual for its plain massive look in this great age of Rococo decoration in Philadelphia. It is uncertain what kind of furniture Gostelowe made before the Revolutionary War, but when he got back to business after it in 1783 he had a label printed which has been found on only four pieces, three of which are chests of drawers. The chief characteristics of two of those chests are their serpentine-shaped fronts, heavy three-sectioned ogee bracket feet and canted front corners. Some fifteen similar chests are now attributed to Gostelowe on the basis of their similarity to the labelled pair and to a famous wedding chest, which from strong documentary evidence was made by Gostelowe for his second wife in 1789. The wedding chest and a diminutive matching dressing stand with the same serpentine-shaped front are part of Yale University's collection.

Gostelowe is almost as famous for his part in the Revolutionary War as for his furniture-making. Like many another Philadelphian he is known to have experimented with the making of nitre or saltpetre, one of the ingredients of gunpowder. On 4th July 1788, as chairman of the Gentleman Cabinet and Chair Maker's Organization, he was at the head of his contingent in the most famous parade in American history, the Federal Procession to celebrate the ratification of the new Constitution by the necessary ten states.

Less well-known Philadelphian craftsmen with reputations perhaps still to be established are George Claypoole, to whom Gostelowe was apprenticed, Edward Duffield, James Gillingham, Jonathan Shoemaker, Daniel Trotter, Thomas Tufft and Jacob Wayne – and Uncle Tom Cobbleigh and all! Philadelphia training is evident in the work of Eliphalet Chapin who worked mainly in Connecticut and in cherry.

Some twenty of the members of the Goddard/Townsend tribe in Newport were cabinetmakers, but labelled work of only three of them is known – that of Job Townsend (1699–1765), his nephew John Townsend (1732–1809), and his son-in-law John Goddard (1723–85). This group though, as mentioned earlier (page 50), is credited with inventing and refining the block-and-shell style for which Newport is famous.

As Quakers and therefore pacifists and with suspected Royalist sympathies anyhow, the Goddards and Townsends took no part in the War. One of John Goddard's brothers returned to England, in fact, and may have taken some good family-made pieces with him. John Goddard himself died heavily in debt as a result of the business dislocation caused by the war. John Townsend worked on in the new Federal style. Furniture from Newport used to be all attributed to the Goddard/Townsends – if it was good – but is now more cautiously dubbed 'school of Goddard/Townsend'. As mentioned earlier, it seems more than likely that other craftsmen working in Newport will eventually be shown to have been as skilful as the G/T group.

Benjamin Frothingham (1734–1809) who worked mainly in Charlestown, Massachusetts, is like Jonathan Gostelowe, almost as famous for his part in the

62 *Block fronted mahogany chest-on-chest with shell carvings, attributed to the Goddard/Townsend group of craftsmen in Newport, Rhode Island. Henry Francis du Pont Winterthur Museum, Delaware.*

63 *A fine Philadelphia mahogany highboy of 1765–75.*
American Museum, Bath.

64 *Mahogany secretary with block front drawers from*
Massachusetts. Note, among other things, the open flame
finials.

67

War and his friendship with George Washington as for his furniture-making. Ten labelled or signed pieces show him working in Queen Anne, Chippendale and Federal styles. One of the key features of his work at this time is an oxbox or reverse serpentine construction in combination with blocking on the lower part of such pieces as slant-top desks, chests-on-chests and secretaries.

The only big name to come out of the South so far is Thomas Elfe, of Charleston, who seems to have run a very large cabinetmaking establishment. A special feature of his work, often noted in his account book as an extra charge is an applied fret, 'double chest of drawers with fret around', 'mahogany bookcase pediment head with a fret'.

65 *A rare mahogany side table thought to have been made by Thomas Affleck, an immigrant craftsman to Philadelphia in the late 1760s. It has Marlborough block feet and delicate lozenge and oval fret carving and is only one of its kind known on this side of the Atlantic. The piece is presently on display in the John Quincy Adams Room at the State Department in Washington.*

66 *Pennsylvania German chest.*

67 *Mahogany chest of drawers with serpentine front, three-sectioned ogee bracket feet and canted front corners decorated with fluting, all typical characteristics of the work of Philadelphia craftsman Jonathan Gostelowe.*

The Federal Period 1790-1825

By 1790 battles had been lost and won. The thirteen colonies had formed a new Republic with a new Constitution and a new President, and along about the same time they also got a new furniture style.

Despite the hostilities and the distasteful notions of taxation and trade restrictions associated with British imports, furniture continued to be imported from Britain during the War years and in increasing quantities after peace was established in 1783. And with the furniture came the latest pattern books, principally George Hepplewhite's *Cabinet-maker and Upholsterer's Guide* (1788) and Thomas Sheraton's *Cabinet-maker and Upholsterer's Drawing Book* (1791–4) on which the style of this period is based. The original inspiration for Hepplewhite's and Sheraton's ideas, though, was roughly speaking classical Rome, and for that reason, apart from the powerful dictates of fashion, the new style was particularly appealing to those who had themselves looked to the republic on the Tiber for inspiration in founding a new state.

A later element in the style of this period, which is found only in the work of New York cabinetmaker Duncan Phyfe, remained basically inspired by Greek and Roman ideas with a dash of ancient Egypt, but was this time filtered principally through what is called the French *Directoire* style, although some English Regency touches–Beau Brummel and all that–have also been detected. The French name is given to the furniture produced in that country between 1792 and 1804, although the republican government that bore the name–it had five directors in the executive branch–was only in office for four of the years concerned,

68 *The Music Room in the Bayou Bend Collection at the Houston Museum of Fine Arts, Texas. The handsome mahogany and satinwood veneered piano case is attributed to Duncan Phyfe of New York. The maple chairs are of the* klismos *type and have painted landscapes across the back rail.*

1795–9. The style was really an overture to the Napoleonic Empire that followed it.

During some seven years of fighting, Newport in particular had suffered from British occupation and a blockade of trade, and never again dominated the furniture business, although good work continued to be done there in the new style.

In Salem, on the other hand, a period of maritime glory began in the 1780s with the opening up of trade with China. Extraordinary wealth was amassed by Salem merchants and sea captains and their fleets of schooners racing around the world. Merchants in the Far East were said to think of Salem as some separate and fabulously rich land, which indeed it was until its trading fleet was ruined by war with Britain in 1812.

The vast wealth accumulated during those years, however, contributed in no small way to the rise of a sophisticated cabinetmaking school in the area, associated with fine mahogany and satinwood. Both woods were readily imported from the East, and it was not long before furniture cooperatives were set up for the export of furniture made from them. Large amounts of furniture were sent out from Salem during these years as venture cargo to be sold by ships' captains wherever they could dispose of it to best advantage–at auctions in the South, at Charleston, South Carolina or Savannah, Georgia, for example, or even further afield in South America, the Madeiras, South Africa or the East Indies. After the discovery of a Salem secretary in South Africa some years ago, who knows how many more pieces are scattered over the face of the globe waiting to be brought home?

Boston and Philadelphia managed to retain their standing as centres of furniture-making and competitors to be reckoned with, despite the troubles. Until quite recently, however, the furniture made there during this period has been overshadowed not only by Salem work, but also by that of the new star, New York, and of an even newer one, Baltimore. New York profited by being the first Federal capital and, as mentioned earlier, assumed a leadership in design and manufacture that it would never relinquish.

Baltimore ('a nest of pirates'–in the eyes of the British, need it be said?) also profited by the years of unrest, and its prosperity boomed as its rivals further up the east coast were hurt by British occupation. The Federal Government had briefly taken refuge there from Philadelphia, and when that Government was finally established in Washington, Baltimore was a handy shopping centre. Thousands of immigrants, many of them trained craftsmen, more than doubled the town's population between 1790 and 1800, and almost overnight, just like Philadelphia before it, Baltimore became a prosperous industrial centre.

In recent research it is felt that too many pieces have been attributed to Baltimore work for want of better information, and that much of it might well have been made in the older cabinetmaking establishments in Philadelphia and further south. But considerable mystery still hangs over southern work, and much re-

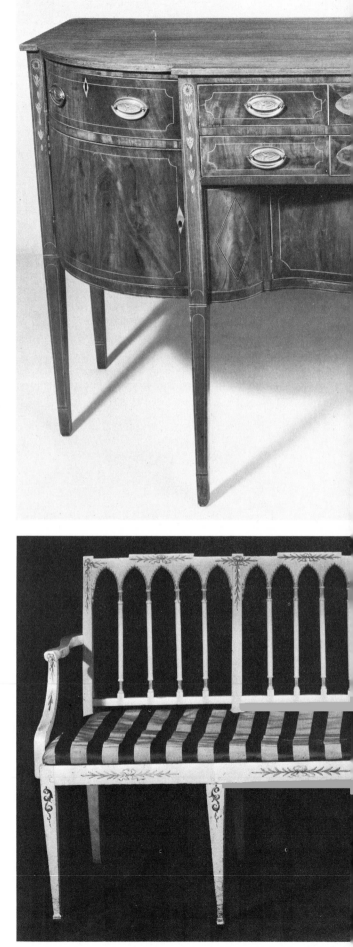

69

70

71

69 *Mahogany sideboard attributed to Nehemiah Adams of Salem, Massachusetts.*

70 *Sheraton-style painted white and gold settee with Gothic arches from New York.*

71 *Curly maple sewing table from New England.*

73 Figured mahogany mixing table (a sideboard for mixing drinks) inlaid with satinwood, maple, walnut and ebony. Long thought to be Baltimore work, that attribution has recently been cancelled, but no new one has yet been assigned. Index of American Design.

72 The Green Room at the White House as it probably looked about 1800 when John Adams, the first President to live in the White House, was its occupant.

74 Painted feather-back chair from Philadelphia about 1796. Museum of Fine Arts, Boston (M. & M. Karolik Collection).

75 Sewing table with slender mahogany legs and birch top and sides, made in Salem, Massachusetts, about 1800. The top sides were long thought to be satinwood but, after a minute sample was subjected to wood analysis some years ago, they were pronounced birch. Index of American Design.

73

74   75

mains to be done in the process of re-attribution.

All four towns—Boston, Philadelphia, New York and Baltimore—are known to have exported furniture at this time. An 1821 newspaper advertisement was recently dug out of oblivion, for example, announcing the arrival in the small town of Buenos Aires of the schooner *Sally* with a full cargo of furniture from Baltimore.

Quite radical changes took place in the look of furniture at this time. The sinuous curves that had characterized much of the furniture of the 18th century were more or less out, and straight rectangular lines and more geometric shapes were back in, although on a considerably lighter, more graceful and slender scale than those of the earliest Jacobean period. There was what one expert has described as a certain brittle aloofness about the furniture of the time which was not altogether out of keeping with the spirit of the new Republic.

Carved surfaces give way to flat ones, and the chief decorative devices are now painting, inlays and veneering. Some carving was still done, and particularly well in Salem and New York, but the characteristic motifs are now thunderbolts, sheaves of wheat, baskets of fruit, drapery and vines. A distinctive wheatear or rice carving is found on the reeded foot posts of Charleston high-post beds.

Some high style painted furniture is found at this time, usually called japanned when the colours were applied in varnishes over a painted ground. And a vogue for painted and gilt pieces was no doubt heightened by the preference shown by the early leaders of the new state—George Washington, John Adams, Thomas Jefferson and James Monroe—for French furniture. Panels of painted and gilt glass with allegorical figures are a characteristic detail in Baltimore furniture. Stencilling, too, was often used and seems to have acted as a substitute for the elaborate metal mounts found on European furniture. But all three techniques are more closely associated with the 'fancy' country furniture produced in prodigious quantities until well past the middle of the 19th century, about which more later.

Inlays and veneers are the really important decorative devices at this time, and regional difference have been noted. Plain stringing (that is, thin lines of inlay in lighter or darker woods than the rest of the piece) is common on New York furniture, whereas different kinds of patterned stringing is more often found on Baltimore and Salem pieces. You can watch out for icicle inlays—teardrops in reverse—on Baltimore work, too. They are usually in light woods dripping down the legs of sideboards. A quarter fan inlay is quite common at door corners on New York sideboards. Other inlaid motifs such as bellflowers, shells, eagles and floral and leaf designs are also associated with Baltimore work, but there is some feeling nowadays that more of them were used in Philadelphia work than has so far been recognized. A delightful bellflower or husk and drop motif is also found on Boston work.

The eagle, being the official emblem of the new state

76 *Mahogany lyre-backed armchairs attributed to Duncan Phyfe of New York. Phyfe gave particular distinction to small hairy paw feet.*

77 *Two Hepplewhite-style mahogany shield-back chairs from New England.*

78 *Square-back Sheraton-style chair from New York, with spade feet, and Prince of Wales feathers in the back splat.*

and of its first president, George Washington, was universally popular. One theory has it that the number of stars accompanying the eagle corresponds to the number of states in the union. But it has also been pointed out that an uneven number of stars is rare and that perhaps strict historical accuracy was subordinated to the demands of symmetry.

Patriotism was probably also pandered to by the demands of trade. It is thought that many of the inlays were in fact imported, and it is likely that British manufacturers were just as happy to supply eagle inlays as they were to supply cotton fabrics imprinted with the eagle motif among other popular American subjects.

The principal wood used for veneers was satinwood, but crotch mahogany (that is, the branch cut which has a particularly attractive grain or figure), figured maples and other woods were used. Recent research in wood analysis has shown that a number of very attractive flame-like figures, long thought to be satinwood, are in fact birch. Isn't science wonderful!

Considerable progress has thus been made in analysing differences of detail in the work of the various furniture-making centres, but the distinctions made by contemporaries, as shown by an advertisement in Baltimore in 1817 for sideboards 'of Boston, New York and Baltimore style', remain tantalizingly unclear.

The disappearance of several old forms of furniture at this time is more than compensated for by an increasing variety of new ones.

The highboy and lowboy, which had matured through the 18th century into pieces of such great beauty and the pride of American cabinetmaking, finally went out of style. The chest-on-chest, too, became something of an anachronism, although as mentioned earlier (page 50) two particularly fine examples were made in Massachusetts within this period.

Chests of drawers came back down to reachable–and bending–heights. A bow-shaped or serpentine front relieves an otherwise plain shape. As dressing chests they are occasionally found with an accompanying mirror, although this seems to have been so only in New England.

A variety of side tables took over the functions of the lowboy, but its dining room function was taken over by a completely new form, the sideboard. This piece was made in all the major centres but particularly well in New York.

Another new form at this time is the work table or sewing table, a diminutive but elegant piece designed for the fancy needleworkers of the day. From the price books it was an expensive item from the start, and it was not alone. Inflation seems to have been a fact of life even at that point. New York and Philadelphia prices were higher than London's, and Charleston's were even higher, although the £ was worth less in those places. The currency was changed to the $ in the 1790s.

A big innovation in dining tables was the introduction of the extension, sectional or accordian table. At first it was simply two semicircular end pieces with drop leaves for insertion between them for big dinner

parties. Later the accordian style frame was developed to hold the inserted leaves and slide back together again after the party.

The Pembroke or breakfast table, now more commonly with rounded leaves, was much more widely used than in the Chippendale period, and seems to have taken over the functions of the tea-table. The tea-drinking habit has never really died out in these parts, despite all that fuss over tea in Boston harbour in 1773. But Americans are thought of more as a nation of coffee drinkers, among the milder stimulants, that is, so perhaps there was some backlash after all.

79 *Baltimore ladies' desk made of mahogany and inlaid with bands of satinwood and holly. The source of the allegorical figures in gold leaf on glass panels is not known, but Justice is recognizable on the right and Temperance on the left on the cabinet doors. That might be Moses at the top centre with a couple of saints either side, but no one is very sure who they are. Index of American Design.*

80 *The McIntire Bedroom at the Henry Francis du Pont Winterthur Museum, Delaware.*

81 *Boston rocking chair of 1825–50. American Museum, Bath.*

Card tables–square, circular, tripod and pedestal based–continued in popularity, notwithstanding the legal and moral condemnation of the pastimes involved. As the gossipy Mrs Frances Trollope noted, the old women of a state made the laws, and the young men broke them. The tables are particularly valuable to scholars because they are highly ornamental and many carried labels, thereby providing important clues as to regional preferences in leg-shapes, carving, inlay and veneers.

As in all style changes, the overall shape of chairs was considerably modified. Cabriole legs are out–on all pieces, not just chairs, of course–and straight ones in. They mostly taper towards the bottom and occasionally end in small tapering blocks called spade feet.

77 The two principal shapes for the backs are the shield, heart or oval shape associated with Hepplewhite's
78 designs, and the square shape associated with Sheraton's. A variety of designs appear within the two basic
74 shapes including the so-called Prince of Wales feathers –yes, even in those proud early Republican days. In Philadelphia they seem to have had a preference for carved and reeded spindles in the back, and in several places turned, carved and reeded legs are found.

Duncan Phyfe introduced New York to the aptly named sabre legs and subsequently to the continuous undulating line of the back and seat rail flowing into the incurved legs, which gave his chairs the look of the
13 ancient Greek *klismos* chair, from which the original inspiration did in fact come. Other classical motifs
76 such as lyres appear as the back splats, and an animal's foreleg and paw, said to be an Eygptian borrowing, often gives special distinction to the feet. Drawings exist to show that the architect Benjamin Latrobe designed a suite of furniture with low sofas and chairs based on Greek forms for the White House, which he also had a hand in designing. They disappeared when the House was burnt by the British in 1814.

A curule base is also found on Phyfe furniture, and manages to look appropriate on his sofas but quite dreadful on the chairs–in my not very humble opinion. The curule shape, or Grecian cross as it was called in the price books, consists of two semicircles joined on their curved sides so that one pair of points makes the feet and the other pair holds up the seat. It was apparently based on a Roman magistrate's folding chair. I think it would have been best left at that.

Upholstered wing chairs get new, more ambitious curves to their wings and arms, and a new style of easy chair is found, which seems to have been a New England speciality. This is the lolling or Martha Wash-
12 ington chair–no one knows how it got the names–and it has a tall narrow back and open arms.

The sofa continued to be in style, although it was considered something of a luxury until after about 1825. The rolling camel-back curves of the Chippendale period are replaced by a straighter back and shallower curves. In Salem and New York pieces there is often a narrow carved rail all round. The old Roman banquet couch comes back on the scene, mostly in New York

again. One Rhode Island craftsman, Adam S. Coe, continued to make sofas in the older Chippendale style.

The newest thing in desks is the tambour closing which virtually replaces the slant-top type. It consists of either vertical or horizontal strips of wood on canvas. The name 'tambour', as far as I can tell, derives not from the French for 'drum' but from its usage in describing a palisade or line of stakes protecting an entrance or roadway. The vertical strips slide open horizontally from a centre closing and the horizontal ones usually slide over in an arc or cylinder shape.

Another type of desk also new at this time is the gentleman's or Salem secretary, after its place of origin in America. It has a breakfront, that is projecting centre section, with kneehole space and a drop-leaf writing area. The case top usually has glass doors. It is this piece that has become associated with Salem's venture cargo because one such was found in South Africa some years ago and now resides at the Winterthur Museum.

The names of some forty craftsmen or furniture establishments are known at this time but precious few pieces can be firmly attributed to any of them. The big names of the period are Samuel McIntire of Salem, who is known for his carving rather than construction of furniture, John and Thomas Seymour of Boston, and Duncan Phyfe of New York. There is a surprising lack of biggies in Baltimore and Philadelphia, although for the moment the Finlay (also Finley and Findlay) brothers–John and Hugh–get the credit for elegant painted furniture from Baltimore. A lot of digging around remains to be done before any new reputations can be established.

It seems likely that Samuel McIntire began his career carving figureheads for the fleets of schooners on which Salem's fame and fortune was based, but he became known for the carved decorations he did on the doorways and mantels of houses he designed for Salem dignitaries after the Revolution. Just when he began carving furniture is not known, but there is documentary proof of his having done the carving on sofas and chairs for the house he designed for Elias Hasket Derby, Salem's most important merchant prince. In addition his fame as the carver of the 'masterpiece of Salem', the chest-on-chest made for Derby's daughter and now in the Boston Museum of Fine Arts, has quite overshadowed that of the chest's assumed maker, William Lemon, about whom little is known.

Various pieces of furniture, particularly sofas and chairs, are now attributed to McIntire because of the similarity of their carving to that on the Lemon chest and on the houses McIntire designed. No one seems to know or care who actually made the pieces concerned. The most characteristic motifs in the carving are bowls and baskets of fruit and flowers and cornucopiae spilling out their abundance. A star or snow-flake design in the punched ground behind the carved motifs is said to be another characteristic of McIntire's carving or, more cautiously, of carving done in Salem.

Perhaps the pieces carved by McIntire were made by such known Salem cabinetmakers as Nehemiah Adams,

82 *A mahogany Salem secretary.*

83 *Accordion extension table attributed to Duncan Phyfe, New York's renowned cabinetmaker in the early years of the 19th century.*

Nathaniel Appleton, William Hook, Edmund Johnson or the Sanderson brothers—Elijah and Samuel—several of whom are also known as furniture exporters.

To date it has not been possible to distinguish the work of John Seymour from that of his son Thomas who are known to have been working together in Boston. They are most famous for their tambour desks, only two of which have labels, their use of beautiful veneers such as patterned satinwood and bird's eye maple, and their delicate inlays across the tambour shutters and down the desk legs. The bellflower inlay of three petals down the legs is similar to sophisticated Baltimore work. A semicircular chest of drawers—demilune commode, in high-flown terms—a rarity in American work, is also attributed to them. Their bill for it to the daughter of Salem merchant Elias Hasket Derby has survived.

Duncan Phyfe was for long considered the only cabinetmaker of any worth in New York at this time, and everything of merit was accordingly attributed to him. But in the process of re-assessment that has been going on over the past few decades, Phyfe has been forced to share some of the glory with such craftsmen as Michael Allison and particularly Charles Honoré Lannuier, one of the first of a wave of French immigrant craftsmen who were to set their mark on American furniture during the 19th century. There is some reason to believe that Phyfe gave the family name 'Fife' its Frenchified air for competitive business reasons.

Re-assessment or no, Phyfe still remains the key New York cabinetmaker of the day, and his output during the fifty years or so he was in business seems to have been enormous. Although he worked in the styles associated with all phases of the classical revival, even the Empire style which is considered to be the first of the once-despised 19th-century styles, Phyfe's best work was done in the first twenty or thirty years of the 19th century when he gave special distinction to American furniture in the Hepplewhite/Sheraton/Directoire styles. His pieces are noted for the fine quality of the mahogany he used, and West Indian exporters are supposed to have dubbed their best pieces 'Duncan Phyfe logs'. His most characteristic work was done on chairs, sofas, window benches and tables, but he also made sideboards, piano cases and smaller pieces such as sewing tables.

Phyfe's fame was not just local either. He exported considerable amounts of furniture to the South, and actually made a bed for Henri Christophe, king of Haiti. 'Mr. Phyfe is so much the United States rage,' wrote one New Yorker in 1816 to relatives in Charleston on the difficulties of getting the busy cabinetmaker to make furniture for them.

The 19th Century

In the 19th century, whilst Britannia was mostly ruling the waves, the new American nation was pushing westwards across a continent.

At the end of the hostilities with Britain in 1783, the new state acquired a massive hunk of land west of the Appalachian Mountains as far as the Mississippi, which more than doubled the size of the original thirteen colonies. In 1800 the huge central area from the Mississippi west to the Rocky Mountains, known as the Louisiana Purchase, was acquired by President Thomas Jefferson from Napoleon. Florida was acquired from Spain by President James Monroe in 1821. By 1850, following the acquisition of Texas and other formerly Spanish-held land in the Far West, and the addition of a few little extras on the north-west border with Canada, the shape of the continental United States was completed. The population of the new state had been about 4 million in 1788. By 1900 it had increased some 15 times to about 60 million.

East coast cities, particularly New York, continued to dominate the furniture business for much of the century, but new centres were opening up. One of the earliest was a place called Grand Rapids, not far from the eastern shore of Lake Michigan. Today its name has become synonymous with bad taste and is associated with the worst efforts of mass production and the churning out of reproductions. But in 1876 the Grand Rapids display at the Philadelphia Centennial Exposition was a big hit despite the jeremiads, and the nation trooped to its doorstep to buy its often economic and stylish Renaissance revival furniture.

In the early part of the century an enterprising businessman from Connecticut called Lambert Hitchcock was scouting out the possibilities for selling his furniture 'in the village of Chicago'. By the end of the

84 Shaker asceticism at the American Museum at Bath. Lining the walls with peg boards was a common Shaker practice.

century that village had become a design centre in its own right and, as such, together with the work being done in California, was to have a considerable impact on modern design. But before Chicago and California grew up, places like Cincinnati on the Ohio River west of the Allegheny Mountains, and a place called Muscatine, still further west in the Upper Mississippi valley became important centres of furniture production, making machines do the work of craftsmen.

The styles of this period continued to come out of Europe mostly by way of Britain and France, and until relatively recently they have usually been written off as quite beyond the attention of any upstanding aesthete. Certainly the wild and exuberant mixing of styles that took place during this time, an eclectic wasteland according to its severest critics, is enough to make the most intrepid classifier blanch. Within the last ten to fifteen years, however, at least two major exhibitions have been mounted in New York which have allowed a fresh look to be taken at the products of an ebullient and expansionist era. And it seems that some of them were not so bad after all.

There was much that was 'contrary to order', to use a Shaker phrase, in the main streams of furniture production in the 19th century. The furniture of that ascetically religious sect offers a stark contrast to much of it. But there is more that is at least interesting and at best good than has been commonly thought. As one expert has put it, the designs of some four centuries were often employed 'with considerable imagination and abandon'.

In roughly consecutive order from about 1830 to 1890 there was the last breath of the classical revival known loosely as 'Empire', after Napoleon and all that, and then the less respectable revivals – Gothic, Rococo (our old friend from the 18th century) and Renaissance. But they often appeared simultaneously and overlapped with each other and with such admixtures as English Jacobean, loosely called Elizabethan just to confuse

89 you, three French Louis's – XIV, XV and XVI – and something called 'neo-grec' which was a variation on Renaissance and Louis XVI, with a few Egyptian motifs thrown in, and other exotic influences from the East, both Near and Far. And pushing its way into it all there was cast iron making its debut as a furniture material. I am just going to skim lightly over a few of those developments and finish up with a look at country and Shaker pieces.

86, 87   The Empire style, long tainted because of its heavy
90   lines and associations with mass production, was the first to be restored to a modicum of respectability. Writers began including it at the end of their discussions on the glories of the preceding two centuries, and there is a tendency nowadays to call it 'Greek revival' or even 'late Federal' as witness to its new stature. The later decades and styles of the century have likewise been slowly incorporated into the furniture story.

There are at least two aspects to the Empire style – or at least two that I am going to mention. The first is

characterized by heavy deep carving of acanthus leaves and plumes and diamond-patterned pineapple motifs and twisted reeding, and – most easily recognizable – by large, sometimes hairy, animal-paw feet. The latter can look surprisingly impressive on a suitably imposing piece, but when you find them on a little old side chair you begin to understand why the period was ignored for so long.

The other aspect of Empire dispenses with the carving and concentrates instead on plain surfaces and large pillars and scrolls. One of the best illustrations of that development is seen in the coloured lithograph advertisement put out by the New York firm of Joseph Meeks & Sons in 1833. That broadside gives a good idea of the style and of the most popular furniture forms of the day.

The two names associated with Gothic furniture in America are A. J. Davis and A. J. Downing. It's best just to stick to initials because you'll go crazy trying to remember that Davis is Alexander Jackson, and Downing Andrew Jackson.

Davis was an architect who also designed furniture and Downing a landscapist and tastemaker – he wrote prolifically on how people should furnish their homes. In his estimation the Gothic style was peculiarly suited to libraries, hallways and bedrooms. This after all was the time when it began to be mooted abroad that different historical styles fitted the moods and functions of different rooms.

Some of the best of Davis's Gothic designs are to be found today at Lyndhurst, a Gothic mansion he also designed which stands on a choice site overlooking the Hudson River some miles north of New York. A particularly attractive set of oak chairs has what are called 'wheel' backs, which is actually a decorative use of the rose-window pattern familiar to all cathedral-watchers. The chairs are thought to have been made by the New York cabinetmakers Burns and Trainque, who according to Downing made 'the most correct Gothic furniture . . . executed in this country'.

Other Gothic motifs such as clustered columns, ogival or pointed arches, trefoils and quatrefoils are found on tall cabinet bookcases and some chairs for example. Trefoils and pointed arches are to be seen on a number of otherwise plain chairs in the White House which have become famous because of their appearance in paintings and prints portraying Lincoln and his cabinet room.

The Gothic style of the 1840s is mostly associated with the Hudson River valley estates like Lyndhurst and its neighbours, although some pieces can also be seen in the Natchez Plantation Houses – now preserved in ante-bellum, that is pre-Civil War, splendour in Mississippi.

The Rococo revival spanned the years 1850–70 and was much more widespread than the Gothic. The man whose name is most closely associated with it, John Henry Belter, was a New York cabinetmaker, catering to the *beau monde* of the growing industrial aristocracy in that town.

85 *Bookcase, 1850-style.
Described as 'Renaissance
style' by a contemporary, this
rosewood bookcase-on-a-
bookcase is a fine example
of what is called '19th-century
eclecticism', the big mix-up of
older styles. The legs, for
example, show the return of the
cabriole after a fashion which,
together with the French scroll
feet, the moulding and carving
of the aprons, are 18th-century
Rococo. The pediment, though,
with its arched and seated
goddess either side of an oval
presentation plaque, is
16th-century Renaissance, but
the twisted columns, loosely
called Elizabethan, go much
further back even to Rome, and
also appear on late 17th-century
English furniture! This piece
was made by the New York firm
of Thomas Brooks to contain a
specially bound set of* Birds of
America *by artist/ornithologist
James Audubon, which New
York firemen presented to the
Swedish singer Jenny Lind.
Museum of the City of New
York (Gift of Arthur S. Vernay).*

86 *The Empire-style Red Room at the White House. The round table in the background is a labelled piece by French immigrant craftsman Charles Honoré Lannuier. The rectangular sofa table with gilt winged supports and twist-turned stretchers, a rare form in American furniture, is also attributed to Lannuier. Note the dolphin arms and feet on the sofa on the right.*

87 *The Empire Guest Room at the White House. A sleigh bed was a common style at this time. A gondola chair is in the foreground.*

88 *Lincoln's bedroom at the White House in the 1860s. The furniture shows elements of the Rococo and Renaissance revival styles and some oriental touches in the heavily upholstered chairs.*

Somewhat reminiscent of the high tortoise-shell combs of old Spain, as one expert has noted, the Rococo style heralded the return of the curve, and of lush carving and of cabriole legs with scrolled feet – the toes turned up and over.

The intricate lacy carving of leaves, flowers and fruit that characterizes Belter's work – the extravagant naturalistic ornament of the critics – is mostly executed with vitality and grace. It appears on the sweeping backs of his sofas and chairs and on the other pieces, such as tables, sideboards and whatnots which made up the 'parlor suites' of the day. A whatnot – much more colourful than its French mother and/or equivalent, the *étagère* – is a delightful piece of Victoriana designed to show off shelves-full of artistic but useless clutter.

Belter patented a process for laminating together thin strips of his favourite rosewood – a hard richly coloured dark red wood streaked with black, which gives off a faint odour of roses when cut. The resulting 'plywood' had the strength, pliability and lightness he needed for the curving shapes and ornate carving of his furniture – considered the most elaborate ever made in these United States. It is sometimes said that it is possible to fake Chippendale but never Belter. Well, that was in the days before it was worth trying. With prices rising for all 19th-century furniture, who knows what might appear on the market?

As in the earlier periods there has been a tendency to credit all the best pieces in the Rococo style to one big name, in this case Belter, but as earlier, it is now being learnt that other craftsmen were his equal. Among them were three New Yorkers, Michael Allison, Charles A. Baudoine and Alexander Roux. Baudoine is often singled out for having made a little infringement of Belter's patent on the laminating process. He made the backs of his chairs out of two pieces with a centre joint instead of one as Belter did. Not surprisingly perhaps, given the essentially French inspiration of the style, two men working briefly in New Orleans – François Seignouret and Prudent Mallard – are also singled out for their work in the Rococo style. Mallard was particularly noted for his bedroom furniture. A bed attributed to him can be seen at the American Museum at Bath.

The Renaissance revival was at its height in the 1870s. It can be seen in the angular outlines of such pieces as sideboards, dressing bureaux, large secretaries, chairs, of course, and the central pedestal base of tables. Square or pear-shaped pillars or columns and moulded panels often decorated with bunches of fruit and game are Renaissance inspired as are such details as cabochons. They are the convex oval medallions with plain surfaces, reminiscent of precious stones, that are decoratively placed here and there, but often in the centre of pediments. Small shields were also used in a similar manner. It must be said, however, that cabochons were also favourite Rococo devices, but we're not going to worry too much about that here.

Fascination with oriental designs and forms – and for 'oriental' read 'Near East, North Africa and Far

89 *Secretary attributed to Leon Marcotte who by the mid 1860s was running one of New York's most important cabinetmaking and decorating establishments. An enthusiastic contemporary described Marcotte's work as being 'in the pure Louis XVI style . . . and if not overdone . . . is simply grand'. This piece is part of a bedroom set which belonged to Theodore Roosevelt's mother and is seen here in the room of the New York house where TR was born.*

90 *Empire pier table of about 1830, probably made in New York. The mirror at the back was useful for checking hemlines.*

91 *The New Orleans Bedroom of the mid 19th century at the American Museum, Bath.*

92 *Painted black and gilt stencilled rocker. Index of American Design.*

East'—reached a new peak after displays of all kinds of exotica from those far-flung places had been seen at the Philadelphia Centennial Exposition in 1876. Strictly speaking the Turkish cosy corners and Moorish dens to be found even in modest homes in the last two decades or so of the century belong more to the story of interior decoration than to that of furniture. I find it hard to single out the furniture from the décor and its bewildering assortment of eccentricities that may or may not have come from strange and distant lands. Amidst such impedimenta as hookahs and incense burners and brass trays and piles of cushions and voluptuous draperies and Japanese metalwork, the occasional coffee table with inlaid mother-of-pearl and other incidental pieces of furniture can be discerned, but it seems more than likely that they were imported.

Rooms loosely designated Moorish were known in the homes of wealthy New Yorkers like John D. Rockefeller and William H. Vanderbilt. The smoking room and two others from the former's home are now very colourfully installed in New York museums, but not much is known about who made the furniture or where.

The pieces of furniture that do betray oriental influence are the heavily upholstered, betasselled and befringed divans, stools, ottomans and sofas. But many of those started appearing much earlier in the century. The influence of the upholsterer was so great that by mid century ornamental tassels were even carved in wood down the sides of chairs. The more-upholstery-than-frame look has at least one claim to modernism. It covered up a new invention—the coiled spring—which vastly improved seating comfort.

The principal wood of this period was imported rosewood, but native black walnut was also widely used. The newest thing in materials as mentioned above was cast iron. It was probably first used in America to make heating stoves, but by about the middle of the century it had become very common for hall and garden furniture. The use of cast iron for the structure of the Crystal Palace exhibition halls first in London in 1851 and shortly afterwards in New York in 1853, helped establish its glamour. The new material was not used to blaze any new trails in design. Rococo scrolls are put to ingenious practical use as hooks on a hat and umbrella stand and are part of the overall design with a very popular grape and vine pattern on a garden bench, for example. Gothic arches too were a favourite pattern which can be seen on the backs of benches in the White House grounds. Moorish-looking fringes are also occasionally found on the benches, and a variety of naturalistic patterns formed of oak leaves and branches, ferns and lilies-of-the-valley were popular.

A craze for bamboo, or an imitation thereof, was at its height in the 1880s along with other oriental exotica. It seems to have been particularly popular for bedroom suites. The style of those pieces, however, was strongly influenced by a reform movement about which something brief will be said in the Postscript to this study (page 89).

The other new materials used in Europe in the latter part of the 19th century—bentwood and papier mâché—were not commonly employed on this side of the Atlantic, as far as can be determined, although many European pieces made from them were imported. A papier mâché piano of all things was part of one New York manufacturer's display at the Crystal Palace Exhibition in that city in 1853. It is thought that John Henry Belter may have known of the steam process devised by Michael Thonet in Austria for bending wood into the shapes he wanted, when he—Belter—devised his laminating process. But Belter used the bending to very different effect. Chairs made of antlers or animals' horns were very popular towards the end of the century, when they added one more exotic touch and doubtless evoked life on the open range.

Just how early mass production techniques were introduced into furniture manufacture is still a matter of debate. Certainly a considerable division of labour had been known in the 18th century. One man just making chair legs, for example, was apparently not uncommon, and interchangeable parts are known to have been made for Windsor chairs and for drawer fronts.

In the early part of the 19th century Duncan Phyfe was one of the first cabinetmakers to operate a factory —or at least the beginnings of one: he is known to have had some one hundred journeymen, cabinetmakers, apprentices, turners, upholsterers and carvers under his supervision. And Belter, too, employed as many as forty apprentices in his 'factory'. Handcraft processes were nevertheless still employed by Phyfe and Belter for the sophisticated work such as carving, and it seems unlikely that power machinery was used for anything but the preliminary cutting and planing of woods, at least for the custom trade (made to order, that is), before about the middle of the 19th century.

Early use of power tools, however, is evident in the large thin sheets of veneer common on all 19th-century furniture and used to great effect in the early Federal period by John and Thomas Seymour in Boston. The larger size and thinness of the veneers was made possible by the use of a circular saw harnessed to water power.

Standardization was obviously on its way in 1833 when the firm of Joseph Meeks & Sons published its advertisement showing some forty pieces with their prices. This was the broadside mentioned above in which the pillar and scroll aspect of the Empire style was clearly depicted. That style was further codified seven years later in 1840 in the country's first pattern book, *The Cabinet-Maker's Assistant*. This book was put together by John Hall of Baltimore, who was probably well aware of the ease with which the newly invented steam-driven band saw could cut the curves and scrolls he advocated. Enterprising manufacturers from Boston to New Orleans and west to the Mississippi seized on the designs.

Manufacturers of cast iron furniture were probably among the first to mass produce their goods. Variable

tops and bases for tables, for example, were available to suit a customer's whims and fancies, and benches advertised in Boston or New York were widely copied, even in faraway California.

Credit for the first mass production of furniture in the United States is usually given, however, to Lambert Hitchcock, the enterprising Connecticut businessman who, as mentioned earlier, was found looking over the possibilities for sales in the village of Chicago early in the century. Hitchcock is famous for his delicately painted and stencilled chairs, settees and rockers which managed to combine Federal stylishness with country simplicity. By about 1820 his chairs had replaced the Windsors in popularity and were flooding the country. Other manufacturers made similar chairs, and they were widely used in hotels and on Ohio River steamboats, for example, but Hitchcock is the most famous since he carefully signed his chairs and stuck to a standard model for more than thirty years. Of course his stencilled designs have also been carefully forged along with the precious signatures! All the parts of Hitchcock chairs were machine-made and combined in assembly line fashion into the finished product.

This was true, too, of other types of country furniture usually called spool or cottage. The name 'spool' comes from the bobbin-like shape of legs and the long strips of

93 *The library at Lyndhurst, Gothic revival mansion on the Hudson River some miles north of New York. The furniture shows a mixture of Gothic, oriental and machine-age influences.*

94 *Rococo-style sofa made by John Henry Belter in New York about 1860. Museum of the City of New York (Gift of Mr and Mrs Ernest Gunther Vietor).*

95 *Cast iron Rococo in the garden. Bench made about 1885 now in the Henry Ford Museum at Dearborn, Michigan.*

96 *Advertisement issued by the New York firm of Joseph Meeks & Sons in 1833 showing the pillar and scroll aspect of the Empire style popular at the time. Metropolitan Museum of Art, New York (Gift of Mrs R. W. Hyde 1943).*

applied ornament. Downing recommended this type of furniture for bedrooms, and many such suites were made. Spool furniture is considered the most machine-oriented of all at this time, since it was made possible by the invention of the multiple-bladed lathe, first used for cutting buttons and spools for cotton thread.

In sharp contrast to much 19th-century furniture, but not so distant from some of its country cousins in its 17th-century inspiration is the serenely simple 84 furniture of a religious sect called the Shakers.

The name Shaker or Shaking Quaker was first given in ridicule to the members of the United Society of Believers in Christ's Second Appearing because of their emotional movements during religious services. A handful of them fled persecution in England in the late 18th century and, under the leadership of Mother Ann Lee, established communities of celibate families first in the state of New York, then in various parts of New England and subsequently further afield in Ohio, Kentucky and Indiana. By 1860, when the movement was at its height, it has been estimated that there were some 6,000 Shakers in the United States. The name stuck and the Believers didn't object although they would have preferred 'Alethians' – 'children of the truth'. Today the sect has almost died out, but their

JOSEPH MEEKS & SONS.
Manufactory of Cabinet and Upholstry Articles
43 & 45, Broad-Street,
NEW YORK.

MEEKS & SONS' MANUFACTORY
of
CABINET FURNITURE.

Entered according to Act of Congress in the year 1833 by Joseph Meeks & Sons in the Clerk's Office of the District of the S. D. of N.Y.

CIRCULAR.

THE above constitute but a small part of the variety of Furniture made by the subscribers; it would be impossible to exhibit all the patterns on this sheet, as we are obliged to keep so great a variety, to suit the taste of our numerous purchasers—the patterns in this and foreign countries are so constantly varying, as to render it necessary for us to make alterations and improvements, and we are constantly getting up new and costly patterns, much to the satisfaction of the public, all of which are warranted to be made of the best materials and workmanship, and will bear the makers' card and names inside, as a guarantee to that effect. Our establishment being one of the oldest, and now the largest in the United States, we are able to execute orders, at wholesale prices, to any amount, and at the shortest notice.

No. 1—A Canopy Bedstead............$90	No. 7—A Mahogany Chair, silk seat and back.........25	No. 39—A Library, Secretary, and Book Case............200
Do. do. with Curtain and Top.......$250 to 500	Nos. 11 and 12—Rosewood Chairs and Silk Seats, each.........15	No. 21—A Mahogany End Dining Table $30—three in a set............150
No. 13—A Canopy Bedstead..............100	Mahogany do. hair cloth Seats, each.........12	No. 24—A Breakfast Table.................40
Do. do. with Curtain and Top.......300 to 600	Nos. 7 and 9—Foot Stools, Mahogany, and covered with hair cloth, each.........10	No. 26—An occasional Table................100
No. 15—A High Post Bedstead...............50	Do. do. Rosewood and Gilt, and covered with Silk, each.........15	Nos. 22 and 30—A Rosewood or Mahogany Pier Table, white marble top and columns.....90
Do. do. with Curtain.......200 to 300	No. 17—A Mahogany Sofa, covered with hair cloth..........100	Do. do. do. Egyptian marble............120
No. 5—A Rosewood and Gilt Washstand..........75	Do. do. covered with silk..........150 to 200	No. 25—A Mahogany Pier Table, white marble top.........110
No. 6—A Mahogany Washstand................50	No. 23—A Mahogany Couch covered with hair cloth..........90	Do. do. Egyptian marble top..........140
No. 3—A Damask Window Curtains, each..........200 to 300	Do. do. covered with silk..........140	No. 27, 29 and 32—Mahogany Centre Tables, white marble top, each.........90
No. 4—A French Drapery Ba..oh..............150	No. 39—A Mahogany Sofa, covered with hair cloth.........80	Do. do. Egyptian marble top..........110
No. 8—A Dressing Table....................35	No. 41—A Mahogany Sofa.................100	No. 28—A Mahogany Wardobe................110
No. 2—A Mahogany Chair, hair..............7	Nos. 1 and 9—Piano Stools, Rosewood and Gilt, each.........25	No. 31—A Mahogany Wardrobe..............90

No. 33—A Mahogany Sideboard..........90
No. 43—A Mahogany Sideboard..........130
No. 34 and 37—Mahogany Card Table, each.........50
No. 35—A Double Washstand, with a white marble top...20
Do. do. Egyptian top..........60
No. 36—A Single Washstand, with white marble top.....20
Do. do. Egyptian top..........30
No. 38—A Mahogany Bureau..............40
No. 40—A Mahogany Dressing Bureau........60
No. 44—A Secretary and Book Case..........80
No. 42—A Mahogany Dressing Glass, with brass candle sticks complete.....80

☞ We would observe, that when any Furniture is wanted of the above patterns, by referring to the above table or card, and giving the number of the same, or by giving a description of any other piece of Furniture in our line, to the Proprietors of the above establishment, the orders will be punctually attended to.

JOSEPH MEEKS & SONS.

villages are being preserved and restored as an important aspect of the American heritage.

Almost every type of furniture was made by the Shakers–chairs, tables, chests, desks, cupboards, beds, washstands and numerous other useful household items. According to one mid 19th-century visitor they believed that the designs of their furniture originated in heaven and that they were transmitted to them by the angels. The world might rationalize the Shaker achievements somewhat differently, but there is little doubt that their religious beliefs determined the designs of their furniture which has been aptly described as 'a religion in wood'.

Mother Ann Lee had denounced as sinful indulgence the 'costly and extravagant furniture' she saw during her proselytizing visits to New York and New England homes and called on her followers to fashion 'plain and simple' pieces. Shaker furniture consequently dispenses with the superfluities–the carving, decorative turnings, inlays and veneers so dear to worldly people. In addition, the Shakers believed that the form of each piece of furniture was predetermined by the use to be made of it and, finally, that the harmony and order of the perfect state to which they subscribed was achieved by marrying simplicity and utility to sound construction and perfect workmanship.

The search for simplicity, utility, purity of form and fine workmanship is everywhere evident in Shaker furniture. Dining tables are the long trestle type, designed to accommodate the most people in the minimum of space, but their underbracing is directly under the top so that the space for legs and knees is unobstructed. Sewing stands are equipped with drawers sliding out from either side, so that two sisters could work together. Some 860 drawers were built into the structure of one dwelling house in order to provide 'space for everything'.

At the Philadelphia Centennial Exposition in 1876, Shaker chairs were awarded a diploma and medal 'for their Strength, Sprightliness and Modest Beauty'. The three slats of a characteristic back are slightly curved for comfort, and despite the seeming delicacy of the posts and legs on their chairs 'the largest person can feel safe in sitting in them without fear of going through them', as was stated in one of their chair catalogues.

Only one concession is made to the superfluities in Shaker furniture and that is in the use of colour or paint. Eventually the paint was thinned or stain substituted so that the natural wood was visible. Chairs and stands usually have a cinnamon, russet tawny brown or red hue. Tables, benches, counters, chests, cupboards, desks and boxes might be almost any shade of red, but cupboards and boxes in particular might have a yellow or blue tone. Bedsteads were usually green.

The Shaker ideal of functionalism has a modern ring to it and did indeed find an echo among other reformers in the later 19th century, whose ideas were to usher in the 20th century.

97 Hitchcock side chair. Index of American Design.

98 *Cottage furniture in the guest room at Sunnyside, former home of Washington Irving. The ball and spool turnings down the front edges of the painted bureau were a common feature of country furniture for a good part of the 19th century.*

Postscript

In 1900 *The House Beautiful* proclaimed: 'The day of cheap veneer, of jig-saw ornament, or poor imitations of French periods is happily over.' Since the excesses of what is called historicism--revivals in one form or another--and the often degenerate ornament created by machines never seem to disappear altogether, the magazine was perhaps a little premature. But reform was in the air and had been for some time before the turn of the century.

The word preached in Britain by William Morris, John Russell and their disciples, calling for a return to honesty of expression and medieval principles of construction, was spread on this side of the Atlantic by English architect and art critic, Charles Lock Eastlake. Eight editions of his book *Hints on Household Taste* appeared in America between 1872 and 1890.

Elegant ebonized furniture, 'everything in black and gilt', as Henry James described it, with rectangular lines and flat surface decoration of painting, marquetry and shallow carving--often with a Japanese flavour--was made in accordance with the new philosophy, and made particularly well by the firm of Christian Herter, for example, in New York. But only the very wealthy, like railway tycoon Jay Gould and famed actress Lilian Russell, could afford it. Much more furniture carried the Eastlake name in defiance of the new philosophy. The machines designed to manufacture ornateness could not be allowed to stand idle, so although Eastlake's rectangular outlines were adopted they were quickly covered with patterns and motifs that defy classification.

Meanwhile the search for simplicity, utility and beauty had been taken up by architects, who also designed furniture, in Boston, California and Chicago. In Boston the work of Henry Hobson Richardson in the early 1880s reflected something of Eastlake's theories.

99 Charles Eames lounge chair and ottoman of 1956.

That of the Greene brothers–Charles and Henry–in Pasadena, California, in the 1890s showed that straightforward construction, the use of natural materials and the avoidance of sham ornament and all those revivals could yet produce pieces of beauty, grace and elegance. In Chicago about the same time, the better-known architect Louis Sullivan and his star pupil, Frank Lloyd Wright, were preaching the need for structural integrity and organic design. Their words fell on deaf ears for some time, but Wright in particular gradually asserted his authority and was among the first designers to believe in machine production and, as he put it, 'the clean cut, straight-line forms that the machine can render far better than would be possible by hand'.

Very little good furniture was made in America in the Art Nouveau style that profoundly influenced European work around the turn of the century, although the work of Louis Comfort Tiffany in that style, particularly his naturalistic lamps, won international acclaim. He seems not to have done much furniture.

Whilst the *beau monde* imported its Art Nouveau and tended to ignore the local calls for new art in favour of a new lot of revivals emanating from the *Ecole des Beaux Arts* in Paris, a wider public was harkening to President Theodore Roosevelt's wholesomeness and thoughts of the simple things of life, and buying Craftsman furniture designed by Gustav Stickley and Elbert Hubbard in their respective corners of New York state. The simple, mostly solid oak benches, tables, chairs, desks and bookcases they made were strong and functional with no nonsense, and they were widely copied. One lively commentator predicts that this re-christened Mission furniture will one day be scraped down to the natural oak–it was mostly stained dark brown–and sold as early American modern!

In the early 1930s a new group of immigrant designers sought refuge on these shores from persecution in Germany. The outstanding figure among them as far as furniture is concerned was Mies van der Rohe, already famed as Director of the Bauhaus school of design in Dessau, and subsequently in Berlin, and for the lounge chair he designed for the Barcelona International
14 Exhibition in 1929. Called the Barcelona chair, it was made of chromium-plated steel bars with leather upholstery, and is still manufactured today by the firm Mies founded in collaboration with Hans and Florence Knoll in 1945–Knoll International. The ideas Mies brought with him to America on the use of the springiness of steel, making possible the application of the cantilever principle to furniture and our seeming suspension in thin air, were in time received more hospitably again in Europe.

After 1945 Charles Eames, native-born American, and Eero Saarinen, Finnish-born American, became the country's leading furniture designers–at least of chairs. They were both architects again. Eames' lounge
99, 100 chair and ottoman made of moulded rosewood plywood and cast aluminium with black leather upholstery is known around the world. Saarinen, on the other hand, is perhaps best known for the sculptural quality of his

plastic chairs among which are the self-explanatory tulip and womb chairs. The slender stem support of the tulip chairs had to be made of aluminium, much to Saarinen's chagrin. He wanted his creation to be entirely of plastic. But there is apparently none in existence that is strong enough in the fine dimensions he wanted.

All furniture styles are in some ways derivative. American furniture by the very nature of the beast has been, more than most perhaps, a remembrance of things past. But, as I trust will have been evident from these pages, the energetic craftsmen who were part of the wider energetic nation-building have left a legacy of sturdy, charming, elegant, sometimes exotic, sometimes incredible, but often beautiful, suitable and convenient pieces which are all worth the cherishing most of them now receive.

100 *Charles Eames dining chairs of 1946.*

101 *Wooten Patent Desk showing influence of the reform ideas associated in America with Charles Lock Eastlake. Several famous Americans are known to have sat at such desks, including publisher Joseph Pulitzer, oil magnate J. D. Rockefeller, railway tycoon Jay Gould, and Spencer I. Baird, Secretary of the Smithsonian Institution, who sat at this one.*

The Leading Craftsmen

Connecticut

EAST WINDSOR
Chapin, Eliphalet
1741–1807

HARTFORD
Disbrowe, Nicholas
1612/13–1683

HITCHCOCKSVILLE
(NOW RIVERTON)
Hitchcock, Lambert
1795–1852

WETHERSFIELD
Blin, Peter
worked 1675–1700

Louisiana

NEW ORLEANS
Mallard, Prudent
1809–after 1860

Seignouret, François
1768–after 1853

Maryland

BALTIMORE
Finlay, John and Hugh
worked 1799–1833

Massachusetts

BOSTON
Badlam, Stephen, Jr
1779–after 1820

Cogswell, John
?–1818

Seymour, John
about 1738–1818

Seymour, Thomas
1771–1848

CHARLESTOWN
Frothingham, Benjamin, Jr
1734–1809

DORCHESTER LOWER MILLS
Badlam, Stephen, Snr
1751–1815

HADLEY
Allis, John
1642–1691

HATFIELD
Allis, Ichabod
1675–1747

Belding, Samuel, Snr
about 1633–1713

Belding, Samuel, Jr
1657–about 1737

IPSWICH
Dennis, Thomas
about 1638–about 1692

Gaines, John, II
1677–about 1750

PLYMOUTH
Alden, John
1599–1687

PLYMOUTH and MARSHFIELD
Winslow, Kenelm
1599–1672

SALEM
Adams, Nehemiah
1769–1840

Appleton, Nathaniel
worked during the
early 1800s

Hook (or Hoock), William
1777–1867

Johnson, Edmund
?–1811

Lemon, William
worked 1796

McIntyre, Samuel
1757–1811

Sanderson, Elijah
1752–1825

TAUNTON
Crosman, Robert
1707–1799

New Hampshire

PORTSMOUTH
Gaines, John, III
1704–1743

Gaines, Thomas
1736–1808

New York

NEW YORK CITY
Allison, Michael
?–1855

Baudoine, Charles A.
worked 1837–1856

Belter, John Henry
1804–1863

Lannuier, Charles Honoré
1779–1819

Phyfe, Duncan
1768–1854

Pennsylvania

JONESTOWN
Selzer, Christian
1749–1831

PHILADELPHIA
Affleck, Thomas
?–1795

Claypoole, George
1730–1793

Gillingham, James
1736–1781

Gostelowe, Jonathan
1745–1795

Randolph, Benjamin
?–1792

Savery, William
1721–1788

Shoemaker, Jonathan
?–1793

Trotter, Daniel
1747–1800

Tufft, Thomas
about 1740–1793

Wayne, Jacob
worked 1783–1805

Rhode Island

NEWPORT
Baker, Benjamin
?–1822

Coe, Adam S.
1782–1862

Goddard, John
1723/4–1785

Townsend, Job
1699–1765

Townsend, Job Edward
1726–1818

Townsend, John
1732–1809

South Carolina

CHARLESTON
Elfe, Thomas, Snr
about 1719–1775

*Colonial America in 1725.
The shading shows the
approximate area of
settlement, dominated by
the large towns.*

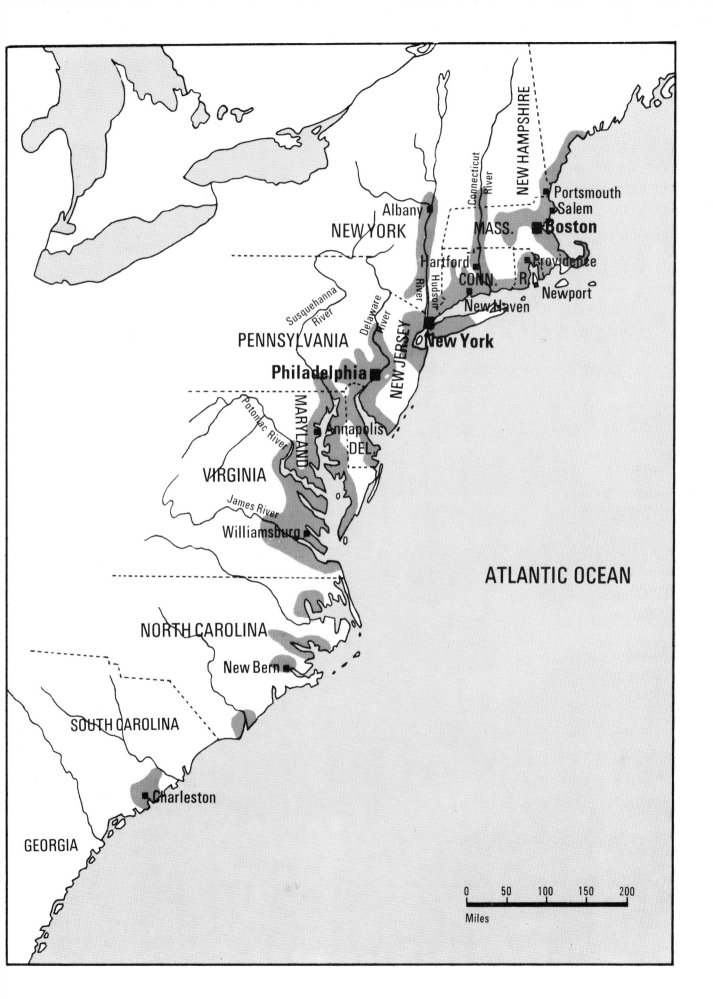

Portsmouth
Salem
Boston
Albany
NEW YORK
MASS.
Hartford
CONN.
Providence
R.
New Haven
Newport
Connecticut River
NEW HAMPSHIRE
Susquehanna River
Delaware River
Hudson River
PENNSYLVANIA
Philadelphia
NEW JERSEY
New York
Potomac River
MARYLAND
Annapolis
DEL.
VIRGINIA
James River
Williamsburg
ATLANTIC OCEAN
NORTH CAROLINA
New Bern
SOUTH CAROLINA
Charleston
GEORGIA

0   50   100   150   200
Miles

Acknowledgments

Photographs were kindly provided by the following:
Colonel and Mrs Miodrag R. Blagojevich 30; Ginsburg &
Levy Inc., New York 10, 53, 56; Greenfield Village and Henry
Ford Museum, Dearborn, Michigan 95; Hamlyn Group
Picture Library 14, 17, 29, 41, 46, 63, 81, 84, 91; Index of
American Design 6, 16, 20, 24, 32, 39, 42, 57, 58, 73, 75, 79, 92, 97;
Lyndhurst/The National Trust for Historic Preservation in
the United States 93; Metropolitan Museum of Art, New
York 15, 27, 31, 34, 51, 96; Herman Miller 99, 100; Museum of
the City of New York 25, 85, 94; Museum of Fine Arts, Boston,
Massachusetts 74; Museum of Fine Arts, Houston, Texas 33,
68; Parke-Bernet, New York 1, 2, 3, 4, 5, 7, 8, 12, 26, 35, 36, 38,
40, 44, 47, 49, 52, 59, 60, 61, 66, 69, 71, 78, 83, 90; Theodore
Roosevelt House, New York 89; Israel Sack Inc., New York 9,
11, 13, 18, 21, 22, 28, 48, 54, 55, 64, 65, 67, 70, 76, 77, 82; Sleepy
Hollow Restorations, Tarrytown, New York 98; Smithsonian
Institution, Washington, D.C. 101; White House Historical
Association, Washington, D.C. 72, 86, 87, 88; Henry Francis
du Pont Wintherthur Museum, Winterthur, Delaware, 19, 23,
37, 43, 45, 50, 62, 80

Index

The numbers in bold type refer to illustrations